Adult
ADHD

"As an empathetic native guide, Hartmann inspires hunters to revel in their evolutionary legacy. He provides empowering strategies for transforming ADHD challenges into tools for prospering in the farmer's domain. The motivating success stories reveal a multitude of paths to self-acceptance and celebrate the triumph of neurodiversity over conformity."

ELLEN LITTMAN, PH.D., COAUTHOR OF
UNDERSTANDING GIRLS WITH ADHD

"My therapy clients often compare ADHD to a radio that is on scan—they jump from station to station and get a lot of static. This book is like landing on *The Thom Hartmann Program* on your radio—a rare voice of calm, clarity, and compassion that reminds us our so-called deficits can often reveal our greatest strengths."

RABBI HILLEL ZEITLIN, LCSW-C,
DIRECTOR OF THE MARYLAND INSTITUTE FOR
ERICKSONIAN HYPNOSIS & PSYCHOTHERAPY

Adult
ADHD

How to Succeed
as a Hunter
in a Farmer's World

THOM HARTMANN

Park Street Press
Rochester, Vermont • Toronto, Canada

Park Street Press
One Park Street
Rochester, Vermont 05767
www.ParkStPress.com

Park Street Press is a division of Inner Traditions International

Library of Congress Cataloging-in-Publication Data
Names: Hartmann, Thom, 1951- author. | Hartmann, Thom, 1951- Focus your energy. | Hartmann, Thom, 1951- ADHD secrets of success.
Title: Adult ADHD : how to succeed as a hunter in a farmer's world / Thom Hartmann.
Description: Rochester, Vermont : Park Street Press, [2016] | Originally published in 1994 by Pocket Books under the title Focus Your Energy: Hunting for Success in Business with Attention Deficit Disorder ; 2nd edition published in 2002 by SelectBooks under the title ADHD Secrets of Success: Coaching Yourself to Fulfillment in the Business World. | Includes bibliographical references and index.
Identifiers: LCCN 2015046074 | ISBN 9781620555750 (pbk.) | ISBN 9781620555767 (e-book)
Subjects: LCSH: Success in business—Psychological aspects. | Risk-taking (Psychology) | Creative ability in business. | Businesspeople—Psychology. | Attention-deficit-disordered adults.
Classification: LCC HF5386 .H27583 2016 | DDC 650.1087/5—dc23
LC record available at http://lccn.loc.gov/2015046074

Printed and bound in the United States by Versa Press, Inc.

10 9 8 7 6 5 4 3 2 1

Text design and layout by Priscilla Baker
This book was typeset in Garamond Premier Pro with Else and Helvetica Neue used as display typefaces

To send correspondence to the author of this book, mail a first-class letter to the author c/o Inner Traditions • Bear & Company, One Park Street, Rochester, VT 05767, and we will forward the communication, or visit **www.thomhartmann.com**.

This book is dedicated to my perpetual partner in virtually all my business enterprises, Louise Hartmann. I have started many businesses that she has ended up managing, always with skill and aplomb. From her I've learned the importance of patience, teamwork, and even the value of boring meetings.

Is It Called ADD or ADHD?

Previous editions of this book used the term ADD (attention deficit disorder). According to the organization of Children and Adults with Attention-Deficit/Hyperactivity Disorder (CHADD), the national resource on ADHD, in recent years "attention deficit hyperactivity disorder," or ADHD, has become the preferred term. The criteria for ADHD and its three different presentations (inattentive, hyperactive-impulsive, and combined) will be discussed in chapter 1.

Contents

Foreword by Michael Popkin, Ph.D.   ix

An Entrepreneur's Note to the Reader
by Wilson Harrell   xi

Acknowledgments   xv

INTRODUCTION How This Book Will Help You   1

TERRITORY ONE

What Is Attention Deficit Hyperactivity Disorder, and Why Is It Important?

1 Nature of ADHD   6

2 Understanding Why ADHD People Are Hunters   12

3 The Challenges of an ADHD Business Hunter   17

4 ADHD Medications and Therapies   20

TERRITORY TWO

How to Succeed with ADHD in the Workplace

5 Hunters within Someone Else's Company   28

6 Succeeding with ADHD in the Workplace   39

TERRITORY THREE

ADHD and Entrepreneurship:
Building Your Own Business

7 The Hunter as Entrepreneur   54

8 Choosing to Start a Business: Your Best Hunt   61

9 Picking Out the Prey:
       What's Your Best Business Goal?   67

TERRITORY FOUR

Hunting for Success:
Building a Life With, Through,
and in Spite of Your ADHD

10 Preparing for the Hunt:
        Ways to Push through ADHD   82

11 Tracking the Prey:
        Heading for Success   94

12 Enjoying the Fruits of the Hunt   110

        Bibliography   113

        Recommended Reading   119

        Index   120

        About the Author   127

Foreword

Michael Popkin, Ph.D.

My mother has a favorite story she still tells friends about when I was a teenager. "His room wasn't exactly messy," she would say, "but he had things lying around everywhere. And when I asked him why, he would say, 'So I know where everything is.'" Then she shakes her head and laughs.

In chapter 11, "Tracking the Prey: Heading for Success," Thom Hartmann makes the observation that "for Hunters, out of sight is out of mind." Ah ha! I knew I had a good reason for my adolescent "organizational system." Now I have a new way to understand why.

In *Adult ADHD: How to Succeed as a Hunter in a Farmer's World*, Thom Hartmann builds on his fascinating theory of ADHD—a theory that turns a so-called disorder into an understandable combination of weaknesses and strengths. Suddenly, ADHD children and adults are not innately defective, they are simply people with the right skills for the wrong time—hunters in a farmer's world. Hartmann's theory puts ADHD in a historical context that we can take pride in, even as it describes how this heritage can prove counterproductive—sometimes fatal—in the business world.

In the same chapter, Hartmann tells me that "a Hunter is visually oriented and aware of everything at once." I flip back to my adolescent room and my visually oriented system. Aha! Another revelation, as my mind springs to my present business. As a child-and-family therapist in private practice in Atlanta, Georgia, I founded Active Parenting Publishers in 1983 to develop the first video-based parent education program. By 1989, my "vision" had become a successful company that was improving the lives of hundreds of thousands of parents and children. We were 243 on the Inc. 500 list of fastest growing companies, and already had innovative video-based programs for self-esteem education, loss education, and teacher training on the drawing boards. My visual orientation and need to see the big picture—those tendencies that my mother still jokes about—had provided the edge to create a winning business.

My years as a therapist working with ADHD children and adults, as well as a host of others with their own weaknesses and strengths, have taught me one powerful lesson: It's not what you have in life that is important, it's what you do with what you have. Thom Hartmann has applied solid principles of psychology and learning in this book to give readers useful tools for doing more with their Hunter strengths, and compensating for those tendencies that have become handicaps in our modern business world.

No one with even a mild set of Hunter genes will escape this book without the kind of Aha! experiences that give us the insight to change our lives. And if you don't find at least a dozen techniques for making you more successful in the business world, well . . . I guess you just weren't paying attention. Fortunately, Thom kept the book brief, which is a good thing, because I'm easily bored. Maybe that's why I make sure our videos are entertaining as well as educational . . . Aha!

Michael H. Popkin, Ph.D., is the author of over twenty-five books and video programs on parenting, including *Taming the Spirited Child* and the *Active Parenting* programs. A frequent media guest, he has appeared on hundreds of television shows, including *The Oprah Winfrey Show,* and on PBS and CNN. He and his wife, Melody, live and work together in Atlanta and are the parents of two young adult children, Megan and Ben.

An Entrepreneur's Note
to the Reader

Wilson Harrell

Every entrepreneur in America must read this book.

For generations we entrepreneurs have been asking ourselves: "Was I born this way, or was it the circumstances of my childhood that led me to the entrepreneurial life? Was it destiny or accident?"

Thom Hartmann has found the answer: most, if not all, of us were born to be entrepreneurs. We are genetically empowered to be what we are.

For me, this was an astounding discovery! Even more mind-boggling is the idea that most of us are "afflicted" with what some would call a "psychological disorder" known as attention deficit hyperactivity disorder or ADHD . . . and it's this very "disorder" that makes us such competent and powerful forces in the business world.

When I read Thom's first book, *Attention Deficit Disorder: A Different Perception,* I went around for days shaking my head in wonder. In that book, Thom went back ten thousand years—before the agricultural revolution—and examined the attributes of the "Hunters" who then inhabited our world. He compared the survival skills of those "Hunters" with today's clinical symptoms of individuals diagnosed with ADHD. They were virtually identical.

The inescapable conclusion: People with ADHD are simply individuals who have inherited a huge dose of "Hunter" genes from prehistoric times. Those genes, of course, are totally different from the "Farmer" genes, which down through the ages have come to dominate the world in which we live.

But that's just the beginning.

In this book, Thom makes another giant leap. He examines the attributes of entrepreneurs and compares them to the qualities of Hunters and the symptoms of ADHD. What an incredible discovery! Entrepreneurs are entrepreneurs because, down through the eons of time, we have inherited the Hunter genes of our ancestors.

The implications are enormous, particularly for those of us who have children. Since entrepreneurs tend to breed entrepreneurs, we are also breeding children with what the schools call attention deficit disorder—and many of those children are now being drugged, at school, every day of their lives. It's a fact. Over five million school children are being drugged so that, while in school, they will stop the Hunter behaviors that might one day make them successful entrepreneurs. Instead they will act like good, compliant Farmer students.

Thom's previous book shows how schools can be restructured to accommodate ADHD children and not just help them to "learn," but also give them the opportunity to excel. In this book he goes the next step, speaking directly to those millions of ADHD/Hunter entrepreneurs, giving specific, usable, real-world techniques and methods to create, build, and maintain a viable business. This business how-to book is different from any that have preceded it, because it is grounded in an understanding of the primal forces that drive our lives. The advice and concepts are not just "good ideas": they're profound truths, necessary for entrepreneurs to be successful over the long run.

For the past six years I have been on a crusade to bring the entrepreneurs of America together. To give them a voice. To make America realize that entrepreneurs—these lonely and terrorized individuals—are creating most of the new jobs in our nation, and are the best hope for our economic future.

Until I read Thom's books, I believed that entrepreneurship was inspired by an insatiable desire for freedom. It's so wonderful to know that it's more, much more. That we are born. That we are genetically bound together. That we can and will pass these incredible genes on to our children and their children's children. That in spite of politicians and Farmer bureaucracies, the entrepreneurial world will live on.

And, lest we forget—thank you, Thom Hartmann, for enlightening our lives.

Wilson Harrell was the former publisher of *Inc.* magazine, former president of the Formula 409 corporation, and one of America's most well-known entrepreneurs. A regular speaker at business events worldwide, he wrote a monthly column for *Success* magazine and was the author of the book *For Entrepreneurs Only*. He died of cancer in 1998—and is sorely missed.

Acknowledgments

Special thanks go to Wilson Harrell, whose enthusiasm inspired me to stop procrastinating and write this book *now*.

Other people deserving thanks are Edward Hallowell, M.D. and John Ratey, M.D. (authors of *Driven to Distraction*), who developed the suggested ADHD diagnostic criteria mentioned in this book; Dave deBronkart who helped in the creation of the core concepts; and those folks who offered encouragement and suggestions, principally Carla Nelson, Mark Powell, M.D., Wendy Hoechstetter, Dirk Huttenbach, M.D., Mark Stein, M.D., Bert Warren, M.D., Mark Oristano, Mary Fowler, Lisa Poast, Mary Jane Johnson, John Paddock, Ph.D., Janie Bowman, Cj Bowman, Dale Hammerschmidt, M.D., Hal Meyer, John and Nancy Roy, Kathy Daya, Carol LaRusso, Joan Lambert, and the many helpful people on the ADD Forum on CompuServe. This book came to fruition through the determined and competent efforts of my agent, Anita Diamant; editors Camille Cunningham and Julie Rubenstein.

My current business associates and friends have all been teachers and helped me form or validate the ideas in this book: Brad Walrod, Jeff Justice, Nigel Peacock, Kathleen Tinkel, David Vining, Don Haughey, Michael Kurland, Susan Barrows, Laura Haggarty, Jim Hart, Ann Linden, Randy Sizemore, Shinji Uehara, Vicki Howard, Todd Gailey, Lamar Waldron, Joe Pruitt, Rachel Ruckart, Deborah Carlen,

Skye Lininger, John Cornicello, Don Arnoldy, Scott Cress, Greg Russell, Patrick Hogenbirk, Steve Zinn, Pat Phelps, Jim Hogan, Dave Eastburn, M. Duke Lane, Dianne Breen, Susan Burgess, Ken Kiyoshi, Rick Bogin, Elisa Davis, Glenda Serpa, Michael Hos, Heidi Waldmann, Nate Lenow, Paul Davis, Massanobu Tanighchi, Martha Swain, Kathy Carlysle, Robert Naddra, Louise Richards, Gerhard Lipfert, Gerda Lipfert, Georgia Griffith, Al Allen, Satya Dev, Tom Rogers, Rick Nash, Bob Koski, Doug Alexander, Ed Lindsey, Sam Olens, Bill Jennings, Michael Armstrong, John Knapp, Brad Doss, Dan O'Dea, Richard Rauh, Ed Brewer, John Hannabach, Gary Grooms, and Tondra Morley. And special thanks to Jennie Marx with Inner Traditions, who did such a brilliant job of line editing and helping with updates to this new and improved version of this book.

And particular thanks go to: Jerry Schneiderman, former business partner and Farmer extraordinaire, who helped me crystallize many of these concepts; my former mentor and business partner Terry O'Connor, who taught me more about business and marketing than any six books could contain; my children, Kindra, Justin, and Kerith, who have taught me so much about life and given me my most important reasons for living; and Tim Underwood, who introduced me to the concept of the methodical Hunter.

To all, I extend my heartfelt gratitude.

How This Book Will Help You

The great direction which Burton has left to men
disordered like you, is this: Be not solitary, be not idle.
SAMUEL JOHNSON, IN A 1779 LETTER TO
LORD CHESTERFIELD, REFERRING TO A QUOTE
FROM AUTHOR ROBERT BURTON (1577–1640)

There is a substantial subpopulation of the world that has a common and somewhat consistent set of personality characteristics. These traits have—for many people—led to difficulties in school, relationships, and work, and are collectively known among psychologists and psychiatrists as attention deficit hyperactivity disorder (ADHD).

When researching this subject I was struck by the number of ADHD adults I met and interviewed who'd chosen to become entrepreneurs, to strike out on their own, to forge their own unique lifestyles and businesses—independent of others. Most often these people are involved in an ever-changing life, often starting many businesses, or regularly leading their existing companies in new directions. They thrive on stimulation, and living "on the edge." One biography of Ben

1

Franklin asserts that he was America's—and possibly the world's—first real entrepreneur, because rather than simply learning a trade and opening a lifelong business, he learned dozens of trades and created more than thirty businesses as well as social and governmental institutions. This creation of something new—over and over again—is the core of entrepreneurship, whether you are a company owner or an "entrepreneur within a company" where your job constantly involves new projects or change.

When writing an earlier book, *Attention Deficit Disorder: A Different Perception,* I heard from a psychologist who specializes in ADHD that perhaps as many as half of all entrepreneurs have ADHD. Now, a few years later and after conversations with thousands of entrepreneurs around the country, I've come to the conclusion that nearly all entrepreneurs have ADHD, to one extent or another.

I'm not speaking here of the fellow who carefully invests his money in a corner dry-cleaning shop, runs his own business on that corner for twenty-five years, to finally retire comfortably. While that person may meet some definitions of entrepreneurship, I'd rather refer to him as an independent small businessperson. Such people constitute an important and stable core of the business life of this country.

Instead I'm speaking here of those individuals who create or participate in dynamic, thriving, ever-growing, ever-changing companies. I'm speaking of the ones who take chances, who experiment: Henry Ford, who had several bankruptcies before he hit on a formula that worked; or Thomas Edison, who tried thousands of different variations before he could get a working lightbulb. These people's lives are often littered with failures, but their successes have given a spark of vitality and enterprise to America, and made our country—particularly in its early days—unique in the world. They continue to bring us innovation and change that give great hope and promise for the future of our nation and the world. Some have applied their entrepreneurial characteristics to become great leaders: John F. Kennedy and Winston Churchill, for example, stand out. Others have created inventions, businesses, social institutions, and art that have changed the world.

This book is about people who have overcome their challenges and in many cases actually used aspects of their ADHD to achieve prosperity or victory, and for those who would seek to emulate them. This book is for those who are willing to take chances, to forge a new niche in the business, social, cultural, political, or art worlds, or to create something new.

And how to do that *successfully*.

In the writing of this book, I've interviewed many people in the business world—including some of America's greatest. Few would want to jump up, raise their hands, and say, "Yes, I have something that psychiatrists call a disorder!" Nonetheless, all were, to my mind, Hunters (my term for people with attention deficit hyperactivity disorder as described in this book) to one extent or another. They shared stories of their successes and failures, from childhood through advanced age, that were remarkably similar.

From these stories, and my own successes and failures as a businessperson and entrepreneur, I've assembled a collection of specific tools and techniques for people with ADHD to achieve success in the business world.

What Is Attention Deficit Hyperactivity Disorder, and Why Is It Important?

Nature of ADHD

It is distraction, not meditation, that becomes habitual;
interruption, not continuity; spasmodic, not constant toil.
. . . Unused capacities atrophy, cease to be.

TILLIE OLSON, *SILENCES*

Attention Deficit Hyperactivity Disorder

We all experience a spectrum of levels or states of consciousness as we go moment to moment through daily life. On one end of the spectrum is a very open, *distractible* state that we experience when driving or walking on a busy street—noticing all the events around us, alert to everything in our environment. At the other end of the spectrum are the *tightly focused* states of consciousness, in which we're so intent on the book we're reading or the conversation we're having that the ticking of the clock in the room, or the drone of traffic, ceases to exist.

When in a normal and relaxed state of consciousness, most people fall into a place somewhere between these two extremes of open and focused. They shift from open to focused and back—with relative ease. It's difficult for the average person, however, to maintain either an extremely focused or an extremely open state of consciousness for hours at a time without such things as meditation training or the use of drugs like caffeine. The natural tendency is to snap back to the centerline between the two states, with a bit of both present.

Some people, however, have an off-center baseline state of consciousness as their norm. Estimates vary between experts and researchers, but these people may represent as little as 10 percent to as much as 40 percent of the population.

About half of these "off-baseline" individuals easily slip into such a focused state that they'll stare at a chessboard for hours on end, or spend day after day dealing with meticulous detail such as spreadsheets, budgets, or complex legal documents. They're rarely diagnosed as having a disorder, because the nature of their deviation from the statistical norm doesn't cause them difficulties in school or work. Who would fault the child who loved to spend hours with his homework, after all?

However, these people may experience some difficulties in their social or interpersonal lives because they become so focused on a single subject that they have little time for anything else. They take no risks, no chances, and think everything out very carefully, often before even speaking.

People on the other end of the spectrum are the subject of this book. Their baseline state of consciousness is closer to the open or distractible end of the spectrum, and they are easily distracted by events around them. They often have problems in school because it is so difficult for them to focus. It's hard for them to push their consciousness into a sufficiently focused state to listen to a teacher drone on for an hour when the kid in the next seat is preparing a spitball or the janitor outside the window is mowing the lawn. They find it hard to work in an "open office environment" where they're surrounded by others, and they need to be able to close the door to get anything done. Their attention span is measured often in minutes, rather than hours. Once they've figured something out, they have no desire to repeat it a dozen times. Their plea is, "OK, already, I'm done with that! What's next?"

These people may have attention deficit hyperactivity disorder (ADHD).

When mental health professionals talk about ADHD, they are referring to a diagnosis based on a specific set of symptoms that cause problems in people's lives. *The Diagnostic and Statistical Manual of Mental Disorders,* published by the American Psychiatric Association (APA), provides the criteria used to diagnose all manner of mental disorders, including ADHD. The fifth edition of this book (called the "DSM-5") was published in 2013. Thankfully, quite a bit has been learned about ADHD over the years, and the diagnostic criteria have changed to incorporate this knowledge. One of the biggest changes is the new focus on adults with ADHD; previously the medical field thought it was just a disorder of childhood.

From the "DSM-5 Fact Sheet on ADHD," developed by CHADD (www.chadd.org):

> ADHD is a neurodevelopmental disorder affecting both children and adults. It is described as a "persistent" or ongoing pattern of inattention and/or hyperactivity-impulsivity that gets in the way of daily life or typical development. Individuals with ADHD may also have difficulties with maintaining attention, executive function (or the brain's ability to begin an activity, organize itself and manage tasks) and working memory.
>
> . . . For many years, the diagnostic criteria for ADHD focused on children as being the ones diagnosed with the disorder. This meant that many teens and adults with symptoms of ADHD might not have been diagnosed, or they weren't diagnosed because the DSM-IV required documenting symptoms before the age of 7. Adults and teens can now be diagnosed more easily because DSM-5 raises the age of when symptoms should be documented. In diagnosing ADHD in adults and teens, clinicians now look back to middle childhood (age 12) and the teen years for the onset of symptoms, not all the way back to childhood (age 7). Additionally, the

new criteria describe and give examples of how the disorder appears in adults and teens.

There are three presentations of ADHD:

> Inattentive
>
> Hyperactive-impulsive
>
> Combined inattentive and hyperactive-impulsive

In the previous edition [of the DSM] the three types of ADHD were referred to as "subtypes." This has changed; subtypes are now referred to as "presentations." Because symptoms may change over time, a person can change "presentations" during their lifetime. This change better describes how the disorder affects an individual at different points of life.

In making the diagnosis, children still should have six or more symptoms of the disorder. In people 17 and older the DSM-5 states they should have at least five symptoms.

The criteria of symptoms for a diagnosis of ADHD:

Inattentive presentation

Fails to give close attention to details or makes careless mistakes.

Has difficulty sustaining attention.

Does not appear to listen.

Struggles to follow through on instructions.

Has difficulty with organization.

Avoids or dislikes tasks requiring a lot of thinking.

Loses things.

Is easily distracted.

Is forgetful in daily activities.

Hyperactive-impulsive presentation

Fidgets with hands or feet or squirms in chair.

Has difficulty remaining seated.

Runs about or climbs excessively in children; extreme restlessness in adults.

Difficulty engaging in activities quietly.

Acts as if driven by a motor; adults will often feel inside like they were driven by a motor.

Talks excessively.

Blurts out answers before questions have been completed.

Difficulty waiting or taking turns.

Interrupts or intrudes upon others.

Combined inattentive and hyperactive-impulsive presentation

Has symptoms from both of the above presentations.*

Psychiatrists Edward Hallowell and John Ratey, early leaders in the adult ADHD community, published the landmark book *Driven to Distraction* in 1994. In their book they detailed the defining characteristics of people with ADHD. Their list provides additional insight into the characteristics of ADHD:

- A sense of under-achievement, of not meeting one's goals (regardless of how much one has actually accomplished)
- Difficulty in getting organized
- Chronic procrastination or trouble beginning a task
- Many projects going on simultaneously; trouble with follow-through
- Tendency to say what comes to mind without necessarily considering the timing or appropriateness of the remark
- A restive search for high stimulation
- A tendency to be easily bored
- Easy distractibility, trouble focusing attention; tendency to tune out or drift away in the middle of a page or a conversation, often coupled with an ability to hyperfocus at times

---

*www.chadd.org/Understanding-ADHD/For-Professionals/For-Healthcare-Professionals.aspx

- Often creative, intuitive, highly intelligent
- Trouble in going through established channels, following proper procedure
- Impatient; low tolerance for frustration
- Impulsive, either verbally or in action, as in impulsive spending of money, changing plans, enacting new schemes or career plans, and the like
- Tendency to worry needlessly, endlessly; tendency to scan the horizon looking for something to worry about alternating with inattention to or disregard for actual dangers
- Sense of impending doom, insecurity, alternating with high-risk-taking
- Mood swings, depression, especially when disengaged from a person or a project
- Restlessness
- Tendency toward addictive behavior
- Chronic problems with self-esteem
- Inaccurate self-observation (both pro and con)
- Family history of ADHD or manic-depressive illness or depression or substance abuse or other disorders of impulse control or mood

So now we have seen what it takes to be diagnosed with ADHD from the medical perspective, but that is not the whole story. How and why did these traits develop in the first place, and to what end?

2

Understanding Why ADHD People Are Hunters

We can change any situation by changing our internal attitude toward it.

DR. HARRY EMERSON FOSDICK

Throughout prehistory, virtually all humans on the planet were members of hunting societies. Then, ten thousand years ago, anthropologists tell us that humanity experienced the agricultural revolution: on several continents people began herding animals or planting crops, settling down, and creating farming societies. This led to a huge expansion in the number of people on the planet, and—like with the industrial revolution—was the force behind the creation of a whole new type of human culture.

But those early, pre-agricultural-revolution hunting societies probably had a unique lifestyle, quite different from that of the farming societies to come and from modern-day culture. There was certainly a different set of cultural norms, and a vastly different type of personality was necessary for survival.

When viewed in an anthropological or historical view, the criteria for diagnosing ADHD could also be seen as characteristics that would be survival skills for a person in a hunting society.

For success in the field, forest, or jungle, a hunter must be easily distractible, constantly scanning his environment. He must be able to juggle many tasks or pursue many possible preys at the same time. He must feel unafraid of taking risks, as risk is the daily life of a hunter. If, after starting after one animal, he sees a better opportunity, he must then quickly (impulsively) have the ability to make the decision to alter course and pursue the new prey. A sense of impending doom would keep him aware at all times of the possibility of predators, and on alert against them. And he would thrive on the adrenaline high of the hunt, while finding boring tasks like cleaning his living area to be so tedious that he'd procrastinate when faced with them. His sense of time would be either very fast or very slow, and he'd be either excited or bored "just by life at the moment."

Characteristics of a Successful Hunter

The most successful hunters of the past (and the present, for that matter) would be classified as ADHD by modern psychologists. And there's growing evidence that, consistent with Darwin's theories, these tendencies are passed from generation to generation, ensuring the survival of future hunting societies. There's even a specific gene that some researchers back in the 1990s believed may "cause" or affect some percentage of ADHD cases. It was first identified several years ago in association with alcohol and drug dependence, and is referred to as the D2A1 variant. It can apparently be transmitted by either the father or the mother, and travels from generation to generation. Since that time, several other genes associated with the neurotransmitter dopamine have been identified—there's extensive information about this in my book *The Edison Gene*.

Farmers, on the other hand, faced different challenges. To live successfully in an agricultural society, a farmer must endure long stretches of boredom and stay put in one place. It takes months for crops to grow, and farmers spend much of that time in tedious tasks of picking bugs off plants or pulling weeds. They may develop good auditory-processing skills through hours of sitting with other farmers and talking to pass the time while the crops grow, or during the winters when the crops are in storage. Their communities would be more social and interdependent.

They cannot afford to be easily distracted, restless, or impulsive: if an impatient farmer were to pull the seedling out of the ground every few days to see how it was growing, it would die. And the Hunter's sense of doom would have to be replaced by a calmer sense of quiet confidence that even though the soil hasn't moved in a week, those seeds are germinating and will eventually break through.

A Farmer's sense of time must be linear and even, and he's only excited or bored when confronted with a truly exciting or boring situation. Unlike a Hunter, he doesn't constantly feel the restive push to hunt, the persistent alert for danger, the internally created sensations of boredom or excitement.

Just as we now have people with all shades of skin, eye color, hair color, and so on as the result of the past years of genetic intermixing, we've also now produced an "averaging" of these two Hunter and Farmer traits, and this has become our "normal" person. But there still remain among us those who are, to greater or lesser degrees, the overfocused Farmers and the highly distractible Hunters.

Why Are There So Few Hunters?

In 1981, when I first put forth the concept that the "symptoms" of ADHD might be vestigial survival skills handed down to us from primitive hunting societies, it was largely a leap of logic. There is solid evidence that ADHD is genetic, and certainly other genetic conditions that are liabilities in modern society were adaptive and aided survival in more primitive societies (such as sickle-cell anemia, which offers some resistance against malaria). But if the "hunting gene" was useful for survival of people with it, why have hunting societies largely died out around the world, and why is ADHD seen only among 5 percent to 20 percent of the population, instead of 50 percent or some other number?

I believe we know the answer to even that last detail.

In the February 1994 issue of *Discover* magazine, the remarkable article "How Africa Became Black" by Jared Diamond summarizes how hunting societies are always wiped out by farming societies over time. It points out that fewer than 10 percent of hunting society members will normally survive when their culture collides with an agricultural society. And it has nothing to do with the hunter's "attention deficits" or with any inherent superiority of the farmers.

The author traced the root languages of the peoples living across central Africa. He found that at one time the area was dominated by hunter-gatherers: the Khoisans and the Pygmies. But over a period of several thousand years, virtually all of the Khoisans and Pygmies were wiped out . . . and replaced by Bantu-speaking farmers. Two entire groups of people were destroyed by the millions, rendering them nearly extinct, while the Bantu-speaking farmers flooded across the continent, dominating central Africa.

The reasons for this startling transformation are several.

First, agriculture is more efficient than hunting in terms of generating calories. Because the same amount of land can support up to ten times more people when farming than if they're hunting, farming societies generally have roughly ten times the population density of hunting societies. In war numbers are always an advantage: particularly in these ratios. Few armies in history have survived an onslaught by another army ten times larger.

Second, diseases such as chicken pox, influenza, and measles, which have virtually wiped out vulnerable populations (such as Native North and South Americans who died by the thousands of measles when they were exposed to this disease by invading Europeans), began as diseases of domesticated animals. The farmers who were regularly exposed to such diseases developed relative immunities. While measles would make them ill, it wouldn't kill them. Those with no prior exposure, however, would often die. So when farmers encountered hunters, they killed them off just by the exposure to their diseases.

And finally, agriculture provides physical stability to a culture. The tribe stays in one spot—while their population grows. This provides them with time to specialize individual jobs: some people become tool- and weapon-makers, others build devices that can be used in war, and create governments, armies, and kingdoms. This gives farmers a huge technological advantage over hunting societies, which are generally more focused on day-to-day survival issues.

While the article points out that "that's not to say that farmers are happier, healthier, or in any way superior to hunter-gatherers," it does go on to show how their greater numbers, immunity to disease, and specialization of jobs will always enable (and, ultimately, cause) them to destroy the hunting societies with which they come in contact.

So now we have an answer to the question: "Where have all the Hunters gone?" Most were killed off, from Europe to Asia to Africa to the Americas. Those who survived were brought into farming cultures either through assimilation, kidnapping, or cultural change—and became the ancestors of that 5 percent to 20 percent of the gene pool with ADHD in Western society.

The Challenges of an ADHD Business Hunter

*It should not be men's acts which disturb us . . . instead, it
is our own opinions of those acts which disturb us.*

MARCUS AURELIUS

Some of the characteristics of ADHD referred to by Hallowell and
Ratey, and by the APA, may not just be the result of genetics or personality type. Instead, such things as poor self-image, problems with
authority, and a low tolerance for frustration may be the result of having grown up in a society—and particularly in school systems—where
Hunter characteristics are punished rather than rewarded.

However, many people with ADHD are successful in the world.
Drs. Hallowell and Ratey point out that they both have ADHD, yet
both also made their way through medical school and into successful
psychiatric practices and the faculty of Harvard.

I gave a speech about ADHD in April of 1994 to the faculty of a
major university in Georgia, and afterward one of the most senior of the
professors of psychology came up to talk with me privately.

"You've probably realized by now that at least a third of the people in this room have ADHD," he said, waving at the roomful of Ph.D.s. "In my opinion, they're among the very best of our professors and instructors. They're constantly noticing everything in the classroom, reacting to the kids instead of just droning on at them, and they keep things interesting."

Another professor, listening to our conversation, later told me that it was her opinion that the movie *Dead Poets Society* (starring Robin Williams) was a brilliant story about an ADHD professor in an institution that couldn't adapt to creative, high-energy people. "That movie had much to teach us all," she said.

Many ADHD adults I interviewed saw their ADHD behaviors as only minor parts of their personalities. On probing, I found that, as children, they had adults (usually a single significant teacher or parent) who believed in them and patiently worked with and through their short attention spans, leaving intact their self-esteem.

Others, however, are the walking wounded, having been battered over and over by teachers, parents, peers, and even employers—who have characterized them as lazy, oppositional, misfit, or defiant. There can be a very real downside to ADHD, as the evaluation of any prison population will show (according to several experts, most people in prison have ADHD). Forgetfulness, disorganization, impulsivity, and boredom (with the substance abuse it often leads to), can all be just as bitterly destructive as constructive. Like the knife that can be a tool of sculpture and creation—or an instrument of death, the characteristics of ADHD can mold or destroy a person's life and career.

Self-knowledge, then, is the first and most important step in turning a disorder into an asset.

According to Mark Stein, M.D., director of the Hyperactivity, Attention, and Learning Problems Clinic at the University of Chicago, where he's an associate professor of psychiatry and pediatrics: "Just having the diagnosis, just realizing what ADHD is and reconciling yourself to it, is 70 percent of the therapy." He points out that this sort of self-knowledge is, in itself, a remarkable instrument of change and empowerment for ADHD individuals.

Similarly Bert Warren, M.D., a physician in New Jersey, wrote to me saying: "I'm a child psychiatrist and haven't treated many ADHD adults, but I made the diagnosis on myself a long time ago and I've made the informal diagnosis on several of my colleagues. It was a great relief to know the diagnosis for all of us, although as practicing professionals, obviously we were competent enough to deal with it. I've been helped by having ADHD in so many ways that the occasional blurting out that I do is negligible by contrast."

As we grow up, our beliefs about who we are, how we fit into the world, and what our capabilities are, are really only stories that we tell ourselves—but they are among the most powerful forces in our lives. These stories begin in childhood with the first comments by others: "What a pretty girl you are," or, "You're a bad boy."

In later chapters we'll discuss the necessity of using this new self-knowledge of our Hunter-like qualities to take control of these internal voices and turn them to positive and supportive ends. We'll rewrite our internal scripts, and learn how to go about reliving them in a practical and powerful fashion.

These are the challenges the ADHD Hunter faces in striking out in a new direction—the distractibility, the feelings of urgency, the impulsiveness and drivenness, the sense of danger. Yet, these challenges can also be tools, which successful entrepreneurs and people in business, the arts, and government have used for hundreds of years to motivate and move them to build great institutions.

ADHD Medications
and Therapies

Coffee, which makes the politician wise,
And see through all things with his half-shut eyes.
ALEXANDER POPE, *THE RAPE OF THE LOCK*

The consensus among most researchers in the field is that attention deficit hyperactivity disorder involves some sort of variation in the chemistry or activity of the brain. Those parts of the brain that control our response to stimuli, the ability to control impulses, and the sense of the passage of time seem to be particularly different from non-ADHD people.

There are a number of ways people alter their brain chemistry, and many of these reduce the apparent effect of ADHD. Exercise, for example, is known to have an effect on how the brain functions, and many ADHD adults I interviewed said that regular cardiovascular exercise was an important part of their lives, producing noticeable changes (sometimes lasting for days) in their ability to focus, think clearly, and control their impulsivity.

The easiest and fastest way to change brain chemistry is through the application of drugs. In our culture, ADHD individuals often use large quantities of caffeine, become easily addicted to alcohol, or even use illegal drugs such as street "speed" or marijuana, in an (often unrealizing) attempt to medicate away their ADHD.

One fellow in his fifties, an attorney and formerly one of the two highest-ranking law enforcement officers in his state, told me that he spent the better part of thirty years drunk (usually secretly, or so he thought at the time) because it "turned off the boredom." Another alcoholic said that when he started using Ritalin, his desire for alcohol went away, because the "internal chatter" subsided.

I was startled to discover that out of several hundred successful adults I interviewed for the first edition of this book (in the late 1990s), nearly a dozen had been smoking marijuana daily for over a decade. It's a habit many started as teenagers in the 1960s or '70s, and they claimed it calmed them down enough that they could function in the workaday world. Now, as marijuana legalization has spread from state to state (both medically and recreationally), I'm finding more and more people who are legally and medically using marijuana as a "treatment" for their ADHD. We're still at a very early stage with regard to its efficacy, but it's at least far less toxic and may have fewer (or, at least, different) side effects than any of the prescription medications used.

Two psychiatrists and a surgeon each separately told me how they used illegal street amphetamines to make it through medical school. Scores of ADHD adults reported how they drink pot after pot of coffee every day, consuming thousands of milligrams of caffeine as a way of making it through the day.

While all of these drugs are used by people in an attempt to self-medicate, none appear to be the most effective medication for softening the effects of ADHD. Plus, the legal and health consequences of such substance misuse or abuse can be devastating.

For those people in the workplace who find that their ADHD symptoms are severe enough to prevent them from being successful, there are several drugs that are more effective and perhaps safer than those mentioned above. Initial experiments on these drugs were performed on children with ADHD, but now—after additional research—many are approved for use in adolescents and adults. Many adults I've interviewed who are taking prescription medications for their ADHD report that the effects are, overall, positive. I have outlined a few options below. CHADD: The National Resource on ADHD (www.CHADD.org /Understanding-ADHD/For-Adults/Treatment/Medication-Management.aspx) has more detailed descriptions of the kinds of medications your doctor might prescribe, as well as the side effects for those medications.

Often ADHD is treated using stimulant medications that increase focus. Some examples are Ritalin (methylphenidate), Adderall (mixed amphetamine salts), and Dexedrine (dextroamphetamine). Stimulant medications do have the potential for abuse, and are considered controlled substances, or "Schedule II" drugs, by the FDA. Stimulant medications for ADHD begin to work very quickly, and are generally only helpful while the drug is in your system.

For years it was believed that there was a "paradoxical effect" that would cause hyperactive children to become calm when given these stimulant drugs, whereas normal children would experience a stimulating effect. This notion has been largely discarded, and the consensus of physicians and researchers now appears that in proper doses the stimulant drugs will increase the focus of anybody, ADHD or not. It's only when these drugs are taken in inappropriately high doses (as is often the case when they're abused) that they produce the wild stimulation, incessant talking, elevated blood pressure, and euphoria that are traditionally associated with "speed."

A fairly new nonstimulant ADHD medication is Strattera (atomoxetine). Strattera is a selective norepinephrine reuptake inhibitor. It takes longer to see the positive effects of Strattera than with stimulant medications. On the plus side, Strattera is effective in the long term, is not as highly restricted a controlled substance, and has limited abuse potential.

Other medications are sometimes prescribed to treat the symptoms of ADHD. Certain antidepressants that affect norepinephrine can help alleviate the symptoms of ADHD; however, they are not specifically approved for treatment of ADHD, and a doctor would prescribe them "off-label" for someone with ADHD. Some antihypertensive medications, as well as wake-promoting agents, can also be helpful.

Many adults I interviewed in the 1990s had been prescribed other psychiatric drugs—including Prozac and Valium—by physicians who had misdiagnosed their ADHD as depression or bipolar disorder. When they received a correct diagnosis of ADHD and changed to known ADHD medications (Ritalin and Norpramine, at that time), they noticed a significant improvement in their condition.

That said, there are two sides to the debate about using drugs to treat ADHD in adults (and in children, for that matter).

The prodrug camp points out that the drugs listed above are generally safe and effective, with fewer and less destructive side effects in most cases than, for example, alcohol or tobacco.

Adults using these drugs—increasingly including marijuana—are often evangelistic in their enthusiasm for them, telling stories of how their lives, relationships, and workplace functionality have dramatically improved. For those people who can't or won't resist using other more destructive or illegal drugs, such prescription substances may even be lifesaving.

The antidrug camp points out that very little is known about the long-term effect of the use of these drugs on adults (particularly the stimulants, which may dispose people over forty to microstrokes that impair memory and function). Because it's been only a few years now that adults have been using such substances for prolonged periods, there is virtually no solid data on the consequences of stimulant or low-dose antidepressant use through middle age and into the later years. What studies were done were done years ago when the drugs were used as diet pills, and led to the government cracking down on the drugs, going so far as to classify Ritalin and the other stimulants as controlled substances, in the same category as morphine.

There have been studies done, however, with other families of drugs that affect the brain, such as Thorazine and the opiate painkillers. These studies show long-term use does, for these drugs, produce long-term changes in the brain's physical structure and its chemistry. The studies on cocaine are particularly distressing, because the brain reacts to cocaine in a fashion so identical to the way it responds to Ritalin and the amphetamines that a cross-tolerance can be measured. (When people use cocaine for a long enough period that they need higher and higher doses to get "high," they then require similarly higher doses of Ritalin to notice any effect from that drug.) Whether these long-term changes are negative, or how permanent they may be, is unknown.

The final side effect of drug use is the most bizarre, and not medical.

Insurance companies report all transactions to a central clearing-house of computerized information, which is then available to all other insurance companies. Often this information makes its way to potential employers or others you may not wish to know you've been diagnosed with and treated for what's labeled as a psychiatric disorder. Some people try to get around this by paying for their doctor's visits and prescriptions with cash, but doctors often report to these same computerized data services, as can pharmacies. And because the stimulants are classified as controlled substances, all prescriptions for them are available to the Drug Enforcement Administration and, through them, to other law enforcement agencies.

Other treatments touted for ADHD include biofeedback, mindfulness training, and meditation; and there's a growing body of evidence that there may be some value to these techniques for teaching people to slow down, focus their attention, and control their impulses. It's still hotly disputed, however, and few psychiatrists would choose such methods over drugs. There are also claims made for herbs, homeopathic drugs, and vitamins, although there is little scientifically sound evidence to back up these claims. Unfortunately, because there's so little profit to be made by researching such therapies, this situation isn't likely to change soon.

Often people turn to psychotherapy to deal with their ADHD. While this is often very useful for dealing with the side effects of growing up with ADHD, such as the damage to self-esteem or the consequences of impulsive decisions, no credible therapist claims to be able to "cure" or do away with ADHD. Because ADHD is rooted in brain structure and biochemistry, the result of our genetic makeup, it's not something that can be "eliminated" by psychotherapy.

The consequences of not recognizing one's ADHD and coming to terms with it can be far-reaching. The two areas where most adults will confidentially report problems both relate to impulsiveness and drivenness, and most often have to do with sexuality or work relationships.

In the sexual area, ADHD adults are often more likely to make impulsive decisions about relationships (including the proverbial one-night stands and office romances), which can—in these days of sexually transmitted infections and lawsuits—be dangerous both health-wise and to one's continued employment (in the case of office romances). They may obsess on a particular person, or feel a drivenness to fulfill their sexual needs that obscures their common sense.

The ADHD-driven need for high stimulation may be at the root of this. Hunters have a built-in need for adventure and require regular rushes of adrenaline, but in modern society such things aren't always readily available. Illicit sexual activity provides this "jolt," which Dr. Hallowell told me is actually—among many of his ADHD patients—a focusing and calming experience. A startling number of adults I interviewed were willing—often even eager—to share these kinds of stories with me, and many said that marijuana or, occasionally, Ritalin, helped them bump out of these obsessive loops and get control of their sex drive. Others talked about working with their spouse to bring variety to their sex life, in an effort to keep them from being tempted to "wander" at the office or while traveling.

In the workplace verbal impulsiveness is also a problem: Hunters often blurt out their thoughts or opinions without first carefully considering the consequences. One fellow told me that after seven months on his first job out of college, he figured he knew better how to run the company than his boss did—so he went to the chairman to point out his boss's failures in logic. He added, "Boy, was I startled when I got the ax." In his second job, although he stayed with the company for six years, "I changed either my job or boss or office or phone extension at least every six months. I stayed with the same company six years, but changed jobs so often that I only had up-to-date business cards about half the time. In one case, for an entire year I just had blanks with the company logo, and hand wrote my name and phone on them."

While this may work for some people and companies, it's probably not a situation even most Hunters would prefer for the long term. For many people, as Dr. Stein points out, just the diagnosis is enough to turn their lives around. For others, exercise, therapy, medication, meditation, or other techniques to work with ADHD may be useful.

How to Succeed with ADHD in the Workplace

5

Hunters within Someone Else's Company

Health lies in action. To be busy is the secret of grace,
and half the secret of content. Let us ask the Gods not for
possessions but for things to do.

WILL DURANT

The vast majority of ADHD adults I've interviewed or talked with over the years have expressed the desire to own their own business, to become an entrepreneur. This is consistent with the Hunter characteristics of resisting authority and structure, craving independence, and possessing a high level of creativity.

But not everybody's cut out for, or even wants, to have her own business. Some Hunters prefer the relative security of working in and for an existing enterprise, or must "keep a job" because of specific life situations. Nonetheless, even in the corporate world, there are many entrepreneurial opportunities.

Years ago a good friend of mine worked as a senior executive for a growing international hotel chain. The chain was buying millions of dollars' worth of furniture and interior decorations, and my friend went to the chairman with a proposal: start a company within the larger corporation to build its own furniture. The chairman, himself a Hunter, immediately saw the value of this and gave the go-ahead. The resulting new enterprise saved the parent corporation time and money, gave them better control over quality and delivery, and allowed my Hunter friend to run his own show, eventually retiring a very wealthy man.

Many companies have the need for this sort of entrepreneurial vision, and it's even become a business fad to "reinvent the corporation" so everybody in the company feels like an entrepreneur. Unfortunately, many of the people promoting this idea miss the fact that most "normal" people don't want to be entrepreneurs. They're perfectly content to work a nine-to-five job and leave the risk to others.

But management that understands the Hunter mind-set—and can identify competent Hunters within a company and give them entrepreneurial opportunities—will succeed in improving productivity.

There is a catch, however, that hooks back to the old cliché about always giving authority to match responsibility. Entrepreneurs, even within a larger corporate context, must run their own show. Those companies that have failed in "entrepreneurializing" their employees have done so because they've retained the top-down power structure while only giving lip service to entrepreneurship within the organization.

The two other most common ways for Hunters to be successful in a corporate structure are to take on jobs in high-stimulation or high-creativity occupations.

Sales Positions for ADHD Hunters

Sales is probably the most common field in the corporate world where we find a high percentage of Hunters. They're drawn to sales: there's always something new, with ample challenge and risk. Sales requires intrinsic motivation and a lot of getting out and moving around. To a large extent salespeople can control their own time, and—it's a hunt!

The place where ADHD salespeople often fall down, however, is in the follow-through.

Numerous excellent books have been written about how to sell. The technologies of prospecting, presenting the product or service, closing the sale, and follow-through are well-known to most people in sales. Win-win selling and other technologies popular in sales self-help books make a lot of sense and work well.

But it's that follow-through after the sale is made, from the filling out of forms to the building of long-term relationships, where most salespeople find their greatest challenge. It's just not in the nature of the Hunter to skin the bear. That's the job for the Farmer-types who stay back in the village and attend to the details of chopping wood, carrying water, and preparing the meals.

Because most sales books don't start out with an understanding of the intrinsic nature of Hunters, they simply offer advice about the importance of follow-through. Knowing, however, that this is actually painful work for Hunters, here's a solution: team up with a Farmer.

Many companies now are finding that a Hunter-Farmer team is the most effective way to sell products or services. The Hunter is responsible for making the calls, doing the presentations, and making the sale. The Farmer organizes the lists of people to cold-call, writes the follow-up letters and sets up subsequent appointments (sales usually take four or more calls/visits), and then forges the long-term relationship with the customer when he finally buys. The Farmer is responsible for keeping the Hunter on task, forcing a daily meeting and evaluating things on a regular basis. The Hunter is responsible for keeping things rolling, maintaining the enthusiasm of the Farmer, getting things started in the company and then handing them off to others, and getting the customers or prospects excited.

This sort of team works well when both people understand their respective jobs, and when their personalities are carefully chosen and compatible. Two Hunters together will be a frenzied disaster; two Farmers together will make few sales. The job descriptions could be called Sales and Sales Support, although a whole range of other descriptions may be appropriate, depending on the industry or profession you've chosen.

Sales management is problematic. Over the years I've hired dozens of salespeople. Most all were Hunters, ideally suited to the hunt of sales, but poorly suited to the Farmer job of management. Yet many, perhaps most, have told me at one time or another that their goal was to end up in sales management.

The problem, of course, is that management of sales is not sales itself. So often in sales-driven companies, however, we see the old Peter Principle at work, where salespeople are promoted to the level of their own incompetence: sales management. Then—when they fail at sales management because the skills necessary to be a good manager aren't built into their personality—they crash and burn, feeling wretched, becoming intolerable, or even losing their jobs.

Management requires attention to detail, patience, never-ending persistence, and a tolerance for boring and repetitive tasks such as planning and budgeting that would (and often do) drive a Hunter to drink. Sales management is no different from any other type of management, except that it requires an understanding of the sales process.

It's unfortunate that in our business culture the most common way to reach higher income and status levels is to move "up" into management. The Army has recognized that some people are very good at doing a particular job, but not necessarily suited for, or interested in, management. To provide these people with an upward career path, they've developed the rank of "warrant officer," which usually doesn't involve any sort of command or administration, but still lets people move up in rank and pay.

Sales is, in and of itself, a noble profession. For a good salesperson it can provide a lifetime of accomplishment and a solid income. Successful sales-driven companies recognize this and provide advancement paths that salespeople can brag to their relatives about—without taking the salesperson out of the field where she performs so well. These include opportunities for increases in pay, as well as new job titles that may have words like "manager," "executive," or "supervisor" in them but don't require the salesperson to manage other people or handle details outside of the sales area. It's not at all uncommon for salespeople in a company to make more than their managers: sometimes several times more. Some companies even reward them with titles like vice president.

Creative Jobs

Creativity isn't one of the APA's diagnostic criteria for the "disorder" of ADHD, but this may just be an oversight on the part of those who created the definition. An inordinate number of people with ADHD seem to be highly creative, and Harvard psychiatrists Hallowell and Ratey even included creativity as one of their proposed diagnostic criteria for identifying ADHD in adults (see chapter 1). While no studies have been done looking for a correlation between creativity and ADHD, many experts on creativity who define the characteristics of a creative person are simultaneously describing, in many ways, a typical person with ADHD.

An ADHD-diagnosed freelance writer told me, "As a reporter, I'm always on the hunt. My ADHD is an asset for me because I chose journalism: it's exciting, it's interesting, and there's not much boredom to it. Every project has a beginning, middle, and end. I can hyperfocus, and then move on to something else." She went on to point out that she's often described by her editors as "unusually creative," and praised for finding new and interesting angles to stories. "I'd notice things that other reporters miss, and the way my mind hops around often leads to new ways of seeing things."

In the advertising field I've met dozens of creative people who are ADHD. The long hair, odd clothes, defiance of business norms, and quirkiness of these people is held out as a badge of honor. When they work with reliable non-ADHD people who make sure the details are covered and deadlines met, the results can be astounding.

In their book *The Creative Vision: A Longitudinal Study of Problem*

Finding in Art, Jacob Getzels and Mihaly Csikszentmihaly assert that the key to identifying creative people is the extent to which they are willing to accept ambiguity in their creative efforts. The book reports a seven-year follow-up study of entering freshman to the Chicago Art Institute who were assessed for their tolerance of ambiguity. Those who could tolerate ambiguity almost up until the finish of whatever project they're working on were also found to be the most creative.

Similarly Dr. Edward Hallowell reports that creativity is a common facet of the ADHD personality in his experience, and even refers to creativity as "ADHD gone right."

The late Michael Crichton, himself a physician and one of the most successful authors of this century, wrote in his autobiography, *Travels,* about his lifelong search for high stimulation, often through travel to distant or dangerous places. "When I look back on my travels," he writes in a chapter titled "Direct Experience,"

> I see an almost obsessive desire for experiences which would increase my self-awareness. I needed new experiences to keep shaking myself up. I don't know why this should be true for me.
>
> In one sense, I suppose the search for new experiences represents an appetite. . . .
>
> I returned to my life with a new sense of balance. I was able to get to the point, to stop spinning my wheels, to know what I wanted to do and how to go about doing it. I was focused and effective.

While his statement doesn't necessarily mean he has ADHD, it is nonetheless a brilliant articulation of the way that Hunters, particularly those who are most creative, use high stimulation as a way of clarifying and focusing their mental and emotional energies.

I recently spent a few days in the home of a writer in Europe who's sold several million copies of his books here in the United States, and listened to him tell in loving detail of his days with the BBC as a war reporter. "I loved being where the action was," he said.

On that same trip, a spring vacation for my wife and two of our children, we decided to shun the normal tourist traps and spent much of our time in Belfast, visiting the poor, war-torn Catholic and Protestant neighborhoods, ever wary of the submachine guns that were so often pointed in our direction. In just the past year, I've been to Kaliningrad, Russia (during the elections there); to a leper colony in rural India during the monsoon; and to the slums of Bogotá, Colombia. Doing volunteer work for an international charity (and writing novels based in these places) gives me the opportunity to regularly get my high-stimulation needs met, while still doing some small good in the world.

Years ago I met a BBC reporter in Klong Toey, one of the most notorious of Bangkok's slums, where he was helping to organize schools and medical facilities for the slum dwellers. He told me, "My drug of choice is adrenaline." A significant majority of the writers and reporters I've known over the years would echo that sentiment.

Many occupations that may not be traditionally thought of as "creative jobs" can be tremendous outlets for creativity. As the university professor who confided to me that he believed the best teachers were ADHD, the teaching profession is a great place for creativity to be used and demonstrated.

Similarly the political arena has its share of Hunters. Former Atlanta city councilman and longtime friend Doug Alexander said, "I hate calling it a deficit or disorder, but that Hunterness quality you describe is important, I think, for success in politics. You have to be noticing things around you all the time, juggling a million issues. There are so many issues and trends buzzing by so fast that if you're not a bit ADHD you'll miss things. Some amount of that Hunter ability to switch from issue to issue quickly is very useful in politics."

On the other hand, Alexander points out, ADHD can be a disaster for a bureaucrat. "They have to attend to the details, the minutia. That's where the overfocused people will do best."

High-Stimulation Jobs

There is a range of jobs available that offer high levels of stimulation and variety, ideally suited to Hunters. In the legal professions these would include being a trial lawyer or litigator, as opposed to a corporate lawyer where you sit and review long documents every day. In medicine a surgeon or emergency care physician or nurse is the obvious choice, as opposed to other specialties where patient care tends to be more predictable and routine. Being a consultant in a variety of fields can also be an exciting arena for the Hunter.

The military also is a place where Hunters often prosper and rise to the top, particularly if their self-esteem and difficulty with authority figures hasn't been damaged to the point where they have problems with the military's caste system. The armed forces provide a well-defined structure that helps people who are generally somewhat disorganized become organized, yet still offers many great Hunter-type jobs. If you've ever talked with a fighter pilot, or even watched the marginally realistic movie *Top Gun,* you know what I mean.

Outside of the professions and the military, Hunters often enjoy jobs ranging from taxi driver to handyman, from teaching to research, from working with crusade-type nonprofits (save the whales, oceans, forests, etc.) to religious evangelism. There also seems to be a preponderance of Hunters in the arts, particularly in acting and performing. The years I spent in radio and TV cause me to realize, on reflection, that a significant number—perhaps a majority—of the "on air" talent I knew were Hunters, as were many of the producers, promoters, PR people, and certainly most of the ad salespeople.

A pilot I interviewed later wrote to me, "My flight instructor was very ADHD. Always disorganized, always late, constantly about ten steps behind the details in her life, kept strange hours (we did many, many 4 a.m. coffee sessions), was impulsive, and highly creative (she's also a writer). But put her in the air, and you won't find a better pilot. She has something like 12,000 hours, ATP, used to be a fire bomber in A-26's, and in general is as competent as anybody I've ever met."

Another pilot said that he thought his ADHD was an asset in the cockpit, because it kept him constantly aware of everything around him:

> I'm probably ADHD (I meet all the diagnostic criteria, in spades), and I have tremendous problems with follow-through, organization, forgetfulness, etc. I was the classic underachiever, dropped out of college, kept being told that I had "so much potential" if only I'd apply myself, etc. You know the litany.
>
> Yet flying is one thing that I do very well. In the cockpit I have absolutely no problems with concentration, organization, or anything. I made top scores on all my flight tests, I've won several air rallies, flown around the country, and I'm constantly getting complimentary comments on my "professionalism" from examiners and other instructors. In my first 350 hours I had one total and one partial engine failure, and both times I found myself hyperfocusing and feeling very calm and competent, and made successful emergency landings.

The common denominator here has to do with recognizing one's Hunterness, and finding a job, lifestyle, profession, calling, or crusade that makes best use of one's strengths. It's wise not to make large demands in the areas where Hunters are weak.

For example, following a speech I'd given on ADHD, a fellow in his early thirties came up and asked to speak with me confidentially. When we were alone, he said, "My name is Don and I've just been diagnosed as having ADHD, and I don't know what to do. Should I take drugs for it?"

Cautioning him that I wasn't a physician, I asked if his ADHD was a problem for him.

"It is at work," Don said. "I work in a small factory doing assembly. After a few hours, I get bored and start making mistakes; my attention wanders easily. I've heard that if I took Ritalin that wouldn't happen."

"That may be true," I said. "What else do you do with your time?"

He leaned forward, suddenly animated. "Well, I skydive. In fact, I'm probably one of the ten best skydivers in the state. I do competition jumps, as well as training other skydivers."

"Is your ADHD a problem there?" I asked.

"No," he said, as if the idea had never occurred to him. "In fact, I'd say it's probably saved my life a dozen times—and the lives of others, too. I'm constantly noticing everything around me, watching everybody. I can't tell you how many times I've helped other people who missed some critical part of the jump."

"You find you're well focused when jumping?"

"Oh, definitely. That adrenaline hit just clears your mind out, makes it clean and strong as polished steel. When I'm jumping out of airplanes is when I feel most alive, most competent. It's something I do very well, and I really love. My wife says I'm addicted to it."

"Have you ever thought of making your living skydiving?" I asked.

Don shook his head. "Yeah, definitely. Last year I was offered a job as jumpmaster with one of the biggest outfits in the state. I'd earn about a thousand dollars a year more than I'm making at the factory."

"Why didn't you take it?"

"My wife said it wasn't a real job. Adults don't jump out of airplanes for a living. She wants me to work a normal, nine-to-five job, even if it's only in a factory." He looked up. "She won't be married to a professional skydiver. Says that's for boys who never grew up."

It was probably the hundredth time that I'd heard that a Hunter adult "just never grew up." Emergency medical technicians, emergency room physicians, fighter pilots, police officers, in-the-field troubleshooters or engineers, consultants, and—of course—entrepreneurs. Over and over again they reported that people around them wanted them to just grow up. Stop taking risks. Stop enjoying all that stimulation. Stop wanting to go your own way. "You've gotta learn to conform, to play the game, to calm down and relax," they're told.

But the true Hunter knows it will never happen.

I've interviewed men and women in their fifties, sixties, seventies, and even their eighties who are still out there running, still leaping from challenge to challenge, still open to new opportunities and welcoming change. They're still in the hunt. They are people poured from the mold of Ben Franklin, who started his thirty-seventh occupation at the age of eighty and, in the last years before his death, took on the British empire as he inspired his countrymen to revolution.

As William James said in an 1878 letter to his wife: "I have often thought that the best way to define a man's character would be to seek out the particular mental or moral attitude in which, when it came up on him, he felt himself most deeply and intensely active and alive. At such moments there is a voice inside which speaks and says: 'This is the real me!'"

For true Hunters in the business world, that voice is a constant validation, a perpetual reminder, and often a driving force.

Succeeding with ADHD
in the Workplace

The virtue of man is measured not by his extraordinary exertions but by his everyday conduct.

Pascal

Should You Come Out about Your ADHD?

One of the basic survival strategies for an ADHD person is to have a quiet place to work. Knowing this, a recently diagnosed ADHD woman told me of what happened when she approached her boss and asked that she be allowed to routinely close the door to her office.

"What are you doing in there that you don't want others to know about?" he asked, implying that she would be making personal phone calls or throwing darts at his picture on the wall.

"I just need a quiet place to work. I can't get anything done when I can hear people out in the hall and in the other offices."

"I have no problem like that," he said. "This is really a weird request. Everybody will think that you're up to something."

"I have attention deficit disorder," she finally said. "I'm easily distracted, more so than the average person."

At first he didn't accept her reason because he knew nothing about ADHD. So she loaned him one of the more popular books on the subject, by a physician who takes a very clinical "this is a mental disorder" position about ADHD. After reading the book her boss made a decision about what to do about her workplace difficulties: he fired her.

Unfortunately he was smart enough to know that he couldn't fire her for having ADHD, as it's considered a disability under federal law. Instead, he collected a dozen small excuses, pushed and provoked her, and finally had enough paper documenting her failures that he could use it to rationalize eliminating the "disordered" employee from his office.

This true story illustrates the risks inherent in "coming out" about ADHD. On the other hand I've talked with dozens of adults in the workplace who are up-front about their ADHD with their employers and coworkers, and have found the dialogue it produces is a benefit. Bringing the subject up leads to ways to help ADHD people be more productive, while helping others understand why sometimes seemingly ordinary tasks (like keeping the desk clean and organized, for example) have always been so difficult for the person with ADHD.

Probably the most common perspective on the issue was shared with me by an ADHD-diagnosed high-school teacher, who's regarded by her peers as one of the most effective instructors in the school. She wrote:

> Since being diagnosed, I haven't told anyone at my school that I have ADHD, although at first I was tempted—I felt almost "born-again!" I did talk with some of the parents of my ADHD students about it, though, and we have gotten into "I think I have it, too" discussions, which are often very liberating for them. (I'm starting to feel a little like J. Edgar Hoover—instead of seeing communists under every chair, I'm seeing ADHD people!) However, I came to the conclusion that it wouldn't be of benefit for the people I work with to know about my ADHD. Few of them fully understand ADHD, anyway, and have that traditional "problem" view of it.

Besides, when I have told few non-ADHD people I have it, they look at me like I've grown a third arm. I don't need that.

Is It Really ADHD?

The subject of coming out about one's ADHD also brings up the issue of how severely affected by ADHD a person must be before he's really diagnosable as—and should have the legal protections afforded to—a person with attention deficit hyperactivity disorder.

Many authors, psychiatrists, and psychologists have become well-known by "diseasifying" people who may be only slightly off from the norm. In her April 10, 1994, article "The Big D Becomes a Trendy Disorder" in the *Sunday Times* (London), author Barbara Amiel laments this trend, pointing out that "Depression is the latest ailment to get its own bandwagon, complete with gala dinners." Similarly there are numerous books to be found that pathologize otherwise normal people who happen to be in relationships with alcoholics, substance abusers, and so on.

Classifying so many people as diseased can easily lead to a cult of victimization, causing people to redefine their own identities as that of the victim—in this case a victim of brain biochemistry. The plethora of books and articles in the 1980s about adult children of alcoholics, or adults who experienced sexual abuse as children, did aid many people by helping them realize that their experience as children was not all that uncommon.

The unfortunate side effect, however, is that such books and articles often also give people license to escape responsibility for their own irresponsible behavior, unproductivity, negative cognitions, and self-fulfilling interpersonal prophesies ("Of course I could only get a C on the test! I'm an ACOA, and everybody knows we are woeful under-achievers," or, "My several marriages reflect the fact that in my alcoholic family I was unable to learn anything about intimacy").

There are certainly millions of people whose lives have been crippled by their ADHD and who have no idea why or what to do about it. On the other hand, there are probably also people who will read this or other books and diagnose themselves, or even seek and receive medication, when their ADHD is really not so severe it should be considered a disorder or disability.

ADHD is not an all-or-nothing diagnosis. There's a spectrum of severity, and a variety of presentations. Some Hunters are hyperactive, while others are so hypoactive as to seem to be passive or daydreamers (see chapter 1).

So, before self-diagnosing and then proclaiming your ADHD to the office, do a reality check with a qualified professional. Contact the child psychologists or child psychiatrists in your area (who are usually the most well informed about ADHD) and ask them for a referral to somebody in their field who specializes in adult ADHD. If you're willing to go on the record about your ADHD, at least be certain first that it's real.

Dealing with ADHD Coworkers

Martha's most common complaint about Bill was that he never did what he said he would. They'd have meetings, go over projects, split up responsibilities, and then go their separate ways. A week later, at the follow-up meeting, Bill always had predictably forgotten several items on the list.

The problem was that Bill, a brilliant and creative public relations person, was an ADHD Hunter . . . and didn't know it. He had learned few compensating strategies for his ADHD, and could never understand how Martha could leave the meeting and remember everything they'd gone over, while he couldn't.

Martha read a book I'd written about ADHD, and—without bringing up the subject of ADHD—simply started asking Bill to take notes during the meetings. At the end of every meeting, she'd ask him to review for his To Do list, and assign specific deadlines to each item. This simple technique solved their problem.

Walking up to a coworker and saying, "I think you have this mental disorder called ADHD," wouldn't make Dale Carnegie's top ten ways of winning friends and influencing people. But it is possible to share with people the strategies in this book, and help walk them through these new systems until they become habits, without ever mentioning ADHD.

Simple things are often the easiest, such as saying to an impulsive person: "That sounds like a good idea, but—before we go any further with it—let's sit on it overnight and then come back to it to see if there may be any other way to improve it." The impulsive Hunter may think you're just being a procrastinator, but with a bit of gentle persuasion, she can often be taught to give her impulses a second view.

If you're a Hunter, and so is your boss, it's particularly problematic. You'll have to work hard to play the Farmer role, or lobby as aggressively as possible to get and keep a real Farmer-type involved in the meetings, work, or processes.

How Can You Be a Good Manager When You're ADHD?

Many bright Hunters are so successful at what they do that they get promoted into management. For a person with ADHD, this can be a mixed blessing: management often requires an attention to detail that's counterintuitive to a Hunter. On the other hand, management may offer new opportunities to use the creativity, leadership, and insight skills that often come along with being an ADHD Hunter (not to mention, typically, a higher income).

The key is knowing what you do well and what you do poorly.

Many years ago I interviewed the CEO of one of America's largest computer companies for an article I was writing for a trade magazine. When I asked him what his personal secret to success was, he said, "My secretary."

I must have looked startled, because he quickly went on to say,

In all my years in business, in each of the large corporations I've been a senior executive with, I've always made the choice of my executive secretary my most important decision. I learned early on that I'm terribly disorganized, I constantly lose things, and if there's more than one project at a time on my desk I get so distracted that nothing gets done. So my secretary, who's actually given the title of executive assistant, is responsible for keeping my schedule, keeping my desk clear, keeping track of all my paperwork and files, and even tells me who to call, where to go, what to do, and when.

He added that she did these things based on meetings the two of them had, and she was helping him follow his own directives, rather than running the show herself.*

This is a theme I've seen repeated—to one extent or another—in the career stories of dozens of successful executives I've interviewed over the years. It's one of the "little secrets" of American corporate culture: the secretary keeps the boss's business life together in the same way her spouse may keep the home and social life together.

Management could be broken into two components: leadership and detail. An ideal manager has both abilities, but ideal managers are very rare. Far more common are the bureaucratic managers who are too detail-oriented for their own good, or the Hunter managers who've risen into management only to find themselves surrounded by responsibilities (like periodic performance reviews) that are boring, stressful, or difficult to remember. Since you're reading this book, you're most likely in the latter category, and for such people the two most important tools are organizational strategies (as discussed later in this book) and a good Farmer assistant or partner.

ADHD need not be an impediment, however, to rising to the heights of management.

---

*This interview was in the 1990s, when the title "secretary" was still common, and almost always applied to women. More than two decades later, thankfully, roles from CEO to "executive assistant" are far less gender specific.

John F. Kennedy's biography by William Manchester, written before JFK's death and with Jackie's assistance, is filled with tales of the president's hyperactivity, his dislike of detail, his inability to keep his desk clean even for a single day, his habit of losing combs and pens constantly, his utter distaste for long-winded people, and his drivenness. When he went off to war in PT109, the Navy was at a loss after the boat sank because, before he left, young Ensign Kennedy had forgotten to post the roster of the men aboard. Yet these symptoms of ADHD didn't prevent him from success, because he was able to surround himself with competent, detail-oriented people (principle among them his brother, Robert, who was the exact opposite personality of Jack), and was willing to delegate to them both responsibility and authority.

Similarly Winston Churchill's parents had all but given up on him by the time he graduated from school. When he was sixteen years old, his mother wrote to him: "Your work is an insult to your intelligence. It is that thoughtlessness of yours which is your greatest enemy."

A few years later, upon his less-than-laudable graduation, Churchill's father wrote:

You [have] demonstrated beyond refutation your slovenly happy-go-lucky harum scarum style of work for which you have always been distinguished at your different schools. . . .With all the advantages you had, with all the abilities which you foolishly think yourself to possess and which some of your relations claim for you, with all the efforts that have been made to make your life easy and agreeable and your work neither oppressive or distasteful, this is the grand result that you come up among the second rate and third rate class. . . . I am certain that if you cannot prevent yourself from leading the idle useless unprofitable life you have had during your school-days and later months, you will become a mere social wastrel, one of the hundreds of the public school failures, and you will degenerate into a shabby unhappy and futile existence. If that is so, you will have to bear all the blame for such misfortunes yourself.

If John Kennedy and Winston Churchill, whose biographies strongly suggest that they had ADHD, could succeed in management, you can, too.

How to Have Successful Meetings

In talking with Hunters in the business world over the years, one comment I hear frequently is how much they hate meetings. Meetings seem like such a time waster, particularly when they're run by an obsessive Farmer. Talk drones on, nobody ever gets to the point, and frequently issues aren't even resolved: they're just discussed.

I've tried many strategies myself over the years to avoid or shorten meetings. They've included insisting that meetings be held in rooms without chairs, that there be absolute time limits (usually fifteen minutes, which is about the limit of my attention span for boring things), or requiring everybody to write down in advance a one-page-or-less summary of their contribution to the meeting and bring it with them.

All of these techniques have helped shorten meetings, but none addressed the point that I was missing, which is that meetings can be of value and just because my impatient nature finds them tiresome doesn't mean they should necessarily be of a length dictated by my biochemistry. Meetings should be as long as they need to be to resolve the issues discussed, and looking back, I realize that I probably missed many important details by imposing arbitrary limits on them.

There are also different types of meetings, ranging from brainstorming to problem-solving to training to organizing to congratulatory. Each has its own needs and structure.

So I've learned some new strategies recently that have allowed me to survive meetings and even make them productive:

1. **The meeting must have a goal, and only one goal.** The person who calls the meeting must define the goal of the meeting, ideally in a single sentence. And, as in good marketing, the goal

should be definable in terms of specific behavior. If the meeting is called to brainstorm a new product name, let's stick to that process and come up with a list of names, but not try to go the next step and work out the details of the product's marketing, or even decide which name is best. Selecting the product name is the goal of the next meeting, as that's a separate process from brainstorming. This keeps meetings to the point, generally makes them shorter, and ensures that their actual goal is accomplished.

2. **The meeting has an agenda.** An extension of the goal, the agenda is written down as a brief outline and distributed to everybody in advance of the meeting. This helps people bring the details, materials, or thoughts to the meeting that will increase its odds of success.

3. **The meeting's focus is maintained.** Somebody in the meeting is assigned the job of keeping things on task and keeping the meeting on focus. This person politely but firmly quashes wandering conversations and digressions, and minimizes distractions. By having agreement at the beginning of the meeting that this is that person's job function, people are less likely to be offended when they wander off into talk of politics or personality or whatever and are corrected and brought back to the topic.

4. **The meeting is summarized in writing.** Somebody in the meeting (usually the person who calls the meeting) is assigned the job of taking notes of the meeting and distributing them to everybody within a few hours of the meeting's end. It's understood that the notes are not to be self-serving or political statements, but simply a terse summary of the actual decisions made or discussion points.

5. **As the meeting goes on, make notes of what you're going to say.** Hunters are often interrupters, and the unfortunate reason is because we know that if we don't blurt it out now, we'll soon forget it. People around us, however, interpret this as egotism:

the interruption says to them that we value their monologue less highly than we do our own words. A simple solution is to write notes of what our thoughts are and what our comments will be. Then we wait for the person speaking to finish, or for an appropriate time, to present what we've written.

6. **Define a structure for the meeting, appropriate to its purpose.** If the meeting is for brainstorming, then the rules of that type of meeting are followed (all ideas are good ideas, no evaluation is done, discussion is free-flowing, things are written on a board or flip-chart so everybody can see them, etc.). If it's a problem-solving meeting, then the formula is usually to define the problem, define the causes, define several possible solutions, and then choose the best solution and determine its execution. Entire books have been written about how to conduct meetings of various types, and I won't try to recreate them here: suffice it to say that meetings should have structure and that different types of meetings will require different types of structures.

7. **Break long meetings into smaller pieces.** If you're essential to the success of the meeting, but it's going to run so long that you'll be tortured by the boredom, suggest that the overall meeting be broken into several shorter meetings. These may be scattered through the day or even over the week. If this is impractical, then try suggesting that there be a five-minute break every fifteen or twenty minutes during the meeting. In addition to helping keep the meeting components to the limit of your attention span, this also often keeps people to the point and promotes brevity.

8. **If the issues are recurrent, consider regular meetings.** By having sales meetings, for example, that run ten minutes every morning instead of a half hour every week, often more work gets done and the meetings aren't viewed as a painful process by the Hunter salespeople. And even the half-hour weekly meeting is preferable to the half-day monthly meetings I've seen some com-

panies have. One key to the success of these kinds of meetings is that the responsibility for holding them is given to a Farmer and never to a Hunter. The former will make sure that they happen, day in and day out, whereas the latter will lose interest after a few days or weeks and what may be important meetings will soon cease to happen.

How Does ADHD Affect Women and Men Differently in the Workplace?

It was once believed that ADHD was a condition that afflicted only boys, and that they grew out of it at puberty. We now know that it's a lifelong characteristic and that it affects women as well as men, in roughly equal numbers.

There's apparently little difference between ADHD men and women in how their brains operate. The differences appear to be more the result of the way we raise little boys and girls, and the types of jobs that women often find available to them in the workplace.

From the point of view of many parents, aggression in boys is a good thing. The old saying of "boys will be boys" shows how our culture has accepted this as a truism, and a few minutes listening to parents on the football sideline as their twelve-year-old goes after the opposing team will quickly validate the notion that we sanction aggression among males.

Little girls, on the other hand, are often taught to be demure and passive. To be boisterous is bad manners, to dress in jeans and play in the dirt is to be a "tomboy," which, in many circles, is a pejorative.

As children enter adolescence, there's the added factor of rising testosterone levels in boys, further increasing their aggressive behaviors.

All of this combines to make the symptoms of impulsivity and impatience far more visible in boys and men, and more characteristic of the way ADHD presents itself in them.

For girls and women, however, the presentation of ADHD is more often in its less forceful forms: disorganization, forgetfulness, and the resulting lowered self-esteem. The Marilyn Monroe or "ditzy blonde" cliché—the woman who can't keep track of her car keys, may be impulsively promiscuous, and sometimes forgets what she's talking about in midsentence—is actually a common presentation of ADHD in women.

The problem for Hunter women in the workplace is that "women's jobs" are often the Farmer jobs: filing, typing, and organizing (often on behalf of ADHD men). While the modern American workplace is certainly changing, and women are coming into nearly all aspects of business life, statistics still show us the unfortunate reality that identically capable women are less likely to have as wide a choice of jobs as men, will have less power or authority in those jobs, and will probably earn less.

Additionally, those ADHD women who seek high stimulation, are high energy, and who are willing to take risks are often labeled with unflattering terms that would not be applied to men. A man of this sort is "ballsy," implying some bizarre sort of virility, whereas a woman who behaves like this is often disliked.

The Hunter president of an advertising agency told me that, in her experience, "Men are shielded more: they're not asked to do as many farmer tasks. Women in the workplace with ADHD can come off as being brash, and some men don't like that. Women can be punished for that. Assertive in a man is bitchy for a woman."

The encouraging news is that as our culture becomes less gender biased, Hunter women are less likely to encounter these useless stereotypes. And as a more thorough picture of ADHD emerges, women who may have said at one time, "I can't be ADHD because I'm not hyperactive," will now realize and come to terms with their Hunter qualities.

The Working Parent— ADHD at Work and at Home

One of the most common reactions I get from parents who, hearing me speak about ADHD, realize that they themselves are Hunters is,

"Thank goodness! I can now stop feeling guilty that I'm not Ward or June Cleaver."

It's difficult being in the workplace, and even more difficult trying to raise a family at the same time. For a Hunter parent, of either gender, the job becomes doubly difficult. (Or triply difficult, if the children are Hunters, too!)

Joan Lambert, a Hunter and freelance journalist, shares what may be the most pithy advice to working parents: Hire a housekeeper to come in one day every week or two.

"So many women I know can keep a lovely home," she says, "but I can't. Understanding my true nature now, I don't feel guilty about it anymore; I accept it. I've given up on cooking and cleaning, and now do what I do well, which is writing. I don't need to have a perfect house."

A single father told me that he enlisted the kids in the housework. Both his sons have their own dirty-clothes baskets, and every Saturday morning they do their own laundry. "It took months to get them to start, but once it became a family ritual, it worked." The three of them take turns cooking and cleaning the kitchen, and everybody is responsible for his own mess elsewhere in the house. "It doesn't always work, so we have a housekeeper come in once a month, but it's better than before, when it was just chaos and the kids expected me to do everything for them."

ADHD and Entrepreneurship

Building Your Own Business

The Hunter as Entrepreneur

Had we lived, I should have had a tale to tell of the
hardihood, endurance, and courage of my companions
which would have stirred the heart of every Englishman.
These rough notes and our dead bodies must tell the tale.

ROBERT FALCON SCOTT (1868–1912),

ENTREPRENEUR AND EXPLORER,

FROM THE LAST DIARY PAGE—FOUND BY

A SEARCHING PARTY IN 1913—OF HIS

TERRA NOVA EXPEDITION TO THE ANTARCTIC

Entrepreneurship

Hunters seem drawn to owning their own businesses. Adults with ADHD are 300 percent more likely to start or own their own companies than are people without ADHD, writes Garret LoPorto in his book, *The DaVinci Method*. There's the thrill of the hunt, of starting something new, of creating from thin air a vital and prosperous enterprise. There's also the lure of not having to dance to another person's tune. The entrepreneur can run her own show, keep her own hours, fashion the business after her own personality. A new challenge—and often a new risk—waits around every corner. Business, when you're at the helm, is one of the most exciting adventures available to modern people in their daily lives.

But there's a trap—a huge pothole in the road to entrepreneurial success—and it's one that sends a majority of people spinning and crashing into the wall.

Build a Business, Not a Job

The trap that many Hunters fall into is that they end up creating not a business, but a job for themselves. They start a company to manufacture or sell a widget, they help make the widgets, and they do the sales. They build themselves so intrinsically into the business that it cannot function without them.

A valid business may be here, many times with a large number of employees, but still the entrepreneur has developed for himself a structure in which he is indispensable. This structure, while necessary in the beginning of a company's life, can be a long-term liability.

In the early stages of a new enterprise, time and energy often are the essential commodities. Money is necessary, certainly, but many fortunes have been built on an investment of just a few hundred dollars. Mickey Arenson built Carnival Cruise Lines by purchasing a dying shipping company for one dollar. Ray Kroc started McDonald's with just a few thousand borrowed dollars. And Andrew Carnegie, who founded U.S. Steel, came to America with less than $25 in his pocket.

In the stories of countless successful (and unsuccessful) entrepreneurs, we usually hear about years of hard work for little money before the company reaches a point where the cash flow will allow for a bit of comfort and some breathing room. This vital ability to bring into the early stages of a business a binge of activity and energy is necessary for the start of most enterprises.

This entrepreneurial stage of a company's life is when the Hunter-Entrepreneur really shines: doing a little bit of everything, always rushing about, attending to a thousand things all at once, all with a mind-boggling hyperfocus.

But then companies necessarily change.

Assuming they haven't failed, they achieve a quiet middle-life stage, when those frantic Hunter skills are less valuable—and may even be a liability. This is the time when it's necessary to draw up budgets based on past activity and project carefully into the future. Management must learn from mistakes and successes to carefully fine-tune the focus of the company. They watch the money and the details with a Farmer's eye, nurturing and helping the employees to grow.

This is the death point for many entrepreneurial ventures, because those midlife corporate needs are totally inconsistent with the abilities of the Hunter who started the company. The boss finds himself rambling around, meddling in other people's work, starting new projects, and taking new risks just for the pure stimulation of it. He diverts precious focus and resources away from activities that the company has already proven successful. Eventually many entrepreneurs kill their businesses by trying to continue on as a Hunter when the company has reached this mature Farmer stage.

The entrepreneur falls into the dual trap of creating a "job" for himself that sticks like glue, and then discovers that the job is no longer fun and probably something that he's no longer even particularly good at.

So, how is the entrepreneur able to avoid the trap?

Successful franchisers—those companies that sell franchises to people who want to own their own small businesses—know a few secrets that the entrepreneur can apply to insure success. By organizing your company from day one as if you were going to sell franchises of it, you'll discover that you're effortlessly insuring your own comfortable retirement. (And who knows? One day you may actually decide to franchise the business, in which case you're way ahead of the game!) This process involves creating a structure for the business that's common to franchises, but usually (and unfortunately) overlooked by entrepreneurs.

Eight Steps to Organizing a Business
If You're an ADHD Hunter

1. Focus the business. From chocolate chip cookie stores to newsletter publishing companies to oldies-only radio stations, this is the age of niche marketing. Companies that find a tight and specific focus for their business will nearly always have a competitive edge over a company with a product or service as one of many peripheral to its primary focus.

This focus may be in the nature of a product or a service, such as creating a school that caters specifically to ADHD children (a great opportunity, by the way). The focus may be on marketing technology, selling price and variety as Wal-Mart does, or selling easy shopping and instant availability as the online warehouse companies do.

Whatever your specialty may be, keep refining it and focusing it more tightly. You can broaden it later, if necessary, or shift to other associated areas if your primary focus doesn't work out.

Franchisers call this the "Marketing Manual." It defines the nature of the company, how it's different from other businesses, what its competitive strengths and weaknesses are, and how the product will be brought to market.

2. Define all the jobs that need to be done—by function. The overall "Management Manual" of a franchise defines on a single page each of the jobs that must be done in a company. Sometimes several jobs will be done by one person, or several people will do one job, but each function within the company needs a definition.

This sounds simple on its face. But the first time I put a company franchise manual together, I was startled by the number of details that I would have otherwise overlooked if I were just writing a general business plan.

3. Write detailed job descriptions that tell someone how to do a specific job—from start to finish. This is a boring, pedantic, and difficult part of the writing process, but an essential step. Breaking it into small pieces, writing one job description a day, or two a week, makes the job easier. Don't overlook the jobs at the top and bottom—who's going to empty the wastebaskets, and how should it be done? Who's going to be the president, and what are her responsibilities?

In each case, when detailing responsibilities—particularly with managerial roles—also specify the authority that accompanies the job. How far can a person go in the independent decision-making process before obtaining additional permission from a superior or from a work group? How much money or resources can a person spend, and to what extent? What guidelines does she need before returning to her supervisor for evaluation or permission?

4. Write a profile of the skills needed for each job. Be very specific here. If somebody is to be a graphic designer for an advertising agency, it's not enough to say, "must have a degree in graphic design" or "must know how to do graphic design." Instead break the job requirements down: must be able to run a Macintosh computer, know how to use Adobe Illustrator and Photoshop, have the ability to create professional-looking designs from scratch, know the fundamentals of design, and so on.

5. Evaluate the list to be certain that a large pool of potential candidates are available for each job. If any of your job functions are esoteric, or require your special knowledge, that should be a red flag. A good franchise can be run largely by high school or college graduates with general degrees, except in those areas where there is a large pool of qualified candidates with the necessary specialized knowledge. If you're going to create a contracting company to build houses, enough electricians are probably in the job pool that losing one won't hurt the company. If you're going to design and build nuclear power plants, though, you may be walking on thin ice when recruiting personnel.

6. Prepare job performance evaluation forms for each position. A supervisor would use this form in a monthly, quarterly, and annual evaluation of each person in the company. Ideally, it should rank the various technical job skills defined above, as well as "people skills" such as enthusiasm, timeliness, ability to work with others, commitment, and so on.

7. Write a summary of how the business operates on a day-to-day basis. Write this in a way that if somebody were to come in cold to run your business, he could do a passable job by just reading this summary. It may only be a few pages, or it may be quite detailed, depending on the type of business you're creating, but in any case it should assume no special knowledge and not use jargon. In the franchise world this is called the "Operations Manual," and is the bible by which the business is run. It also often contains evaluation forms for the business itself to determine whether its goals are being met, both for performance, growth, profitability, and quality of product or service.

8. Write each of these "manuals" in such a fashion that any high school graduate with good common sense could read them, and could then run the business. If any part of these manuals doesn't meet this criterion, consider this a warning that your business may end up becoming a job that will stick to you like flypaper for the rest of your life.

The Coming Moment of Freedom

After this homework is done, you can set much of it aside for the moment while beginning your new enterprise. The exercise makes the project ahead much clearer. If you're the kind of person who can methodically follow a plan, you can even use these manuals now. Most entrepreneurs, however, would shiver at the thought of having to review and fill out such manuals and forms every day or week. Instead they just forge ahead and create the business, doing everything ad hoc.

The manuals will really be useful when your new venture reaches its "middle age" stage, usually after two or three years. Then you'll pull them out, refine them to reflect the business as it's become, and then hire a good Farmer manager. You'll say, "Here's how to run the business, and how I expect you to evaluate the people here, the company, and yourself."

You then become a consultant to your own company, just doing the jobs that you enjoy, such as training sales people, developing new products, making presentations, or working on a project-by-project basis. You make the transition from boss-manager to owner-consultant, or even sell the company and go off to start something new. By setting it up this way from the very beginning, you avoid both the early-on entrepreneurial traps of poor focus and poor planning, and the later-years traps of Hunters trying to do Farmer management jobs.

Choosing to
Start a Business
Your Best Hunt

We never know how high we are
Till we are called to rise
And then, if we are true to plan
Our statures touch the skies.

EMILY DICKINSON

Authors lament that fans are always asking them, "Where do you get your ideas?" Entrepreneurs who have started many businesses are often asked a variation on the same question: "Where did you get the idea for this business?" or, "How did you get this thing started?"

The answer is nearly always that the business started in response to a problem created by a need.

What to Do? What Kind of Business to Start?

One of the most common characteristics of Hunters is that they're very creative people. With free-ranging minds and imaginations, they look at the world through an ever-changing set of perspectives, and they tend to be horizontal—rather than vertical—problem-solvers. This is a powerful gift of nature, and something to nurture through specific techniques that Hunters over the ages have left us. It allows us to beat the bushes of our mind and the world for new ideas, new inventions, and new businesses.

Horizontal and vertical problem-solving have to do with the way that people approach difficulties. A vertical problem-solver, when confronted with a badly stuck door, may push harder and harder. When that doesn't work, he'll run into it with his shoulder. If that doesn't work, he'll try kicking it, pushing harder and harder, but always using variations of the same basic strategy: push on the door.

A horizontal problem-solver will walk around the house looking for another door that may be open, or a window that could be lifted.

While this is a somewhat simplistic explanation, if you start to view how people approach problems, you'll notice that the average person is a vertical problem-solver. When things don't work out, they try harder in the same old ways—until finally they're exhausted and give up. Hunters, more often, are horizontal problem-solvers, and look for new ways to do old tasks. I've met several prolific inventors in my life, and every one has been a classic Hunter; they've trained themselves to look at problems from new directions.

There's an old saying that every problem contains the seed of a new opportunity. Dale Carnegie wrote that when life hands us a lemon, we should make lemonade. While these sayings are in some ways clichés, they're also profound truths.

For example, I owned a business that sold a specific part for a particular type of computer in the early days of the computer industry. My partner in New York shipped the parts, and I wrote and placed ads, wrote news releases, and did presentations at trade shows. One of our most important and cost-effective marketing tools was the newsletter we produced, which I wrote, designed, and had printed locally.

When, in 1986, my wife and I decided to sell another business we owned and retire for a year to Europe to do volunteer work with a charity we'd admired, my partner and I were confronted with a dilemma. While I could still design and place ads from Europe by mail and phone, the newsletter was more complex and dynamic. It needed somebody in the United States to produce it.

So I went shopping for a company that could produce our company's newsletter. What I found first were ad agencies who would charge me thousands of dollars a page for layout, writing, and design. (Since they can get that for an ad, why should they charge less for an even more complex newsletter?) On the other end of the spectrum, print shops with relatively low-wage "Desktop Publishers" in the back room would produce the newsletter for $50 per page, but it would look like the poor-quality supermarket flyers they were used to producing back in those days.

That year our company didn't produce a newsletter. When my wife Louise and I returned from Germany in 1987, we opened The Newsletter Factory, a company that could economically and efficiently produce ad-agency-quality newsletters at an affordable price. We'd seen from our own firsthand experience—our own business problem—the seed of an opportunity.

Create a Business You Can Use

The annals of business success are filled with such stories of people who started companies or invented products because they themselves needed them. Looking at a problem in a new way, asking yourself if there's some other way to solve this problem, and then finding ways to turn that problem into an opportunity are skills that you already possess. They're intrinsic to the Hunter personality.

One of the most powerful ways to cultivate and strengthen your Hunter skills is to make use of daily "quiet time." I was first introduced to this when I learned Transcendental Meditation back in 1968, when the Beatles were studying with the Maharishi—it was all the rage among teenagers. There are many ways and techniques for meditation: these range from reciting a rosary to simply sitting in a chair in the office with the door closed for fifteen minutes each day and "purpose-fully daydreaming."

During these moments of quiet time, ideas bubble to the surface of the mind in an unending stream. Sometimes we get lost on "thought trains" and wander off in strange directions. Wholly unexpected ideas pop up, and new ways to look at things are suddenly apparent.

Because Hunters have been told all their lives that they're lazy or procrastinators, I've found that many are initially resistant to this idea of "doing nothing." So, instead, think of it as an important "job," and assign time for it every day. Tell those around you that it's your work time and you're not to be disturbed, or do it early in the morning or later in the evening (or both).

Record Your Ideas and Visions

It's important to get in the habit of carrying a pad and paper around to capture your ideas, and keep it handy during your quiet time. By writing down an idea, you can release it and move on to the next one. If you come up with a few dozen a week, you'll be amazed at how many are actually useful.

Several Hunters were discussing this technique in the ADD Forum on CompuServe (the international computer network) in early 1993, and they all discovered that they'd been doing the same thing, each thinking that she was somehow odd for doing it, but finding it incredibly useful. Many had picked up small, pocket microcassette recorders to use instead of a notebook, because so many good ideas come when they're driving or during the night, when it's inconvenient to try to write something down.

Several companies sell versions of a ballpoint pen with a built-in digital recorder. You play it back by holding it up to your ear and pressing the button. The prices start at about $20 and go up to $150. This may seem like just another toy to a Farmer, but a Hunter will instantly recognize the value of always having such a note-taking tool available.

(And while some Hunters are constantly losing things like pens and would shudder at the idea of such an expensive one, others have discovered that having a few "expensive toys" like this causes them to be constantly aware of where they are—and they rarely get lost.)

There are also smartphone apps that have been developed to assist Hunters. For example, Eric Tives' article "The 30 Best Apps for ADHD Minds," is available on the ADDitute website (www.additudemag.com/adhd/article/11135.html). He lists his recommended apps by categories including "Manage Information," "Increase Creativity," and "Decrease Distraction," so you can choose apps that address your specific needs.

Procrastination Can Be Good, When Done Right

Recognize that not every idea may be brilliant, but that some will be. Hunters tend to be impulsive, and they get very excited about a new idea, wanting to jump on it right away while their enthusiasm is high. If you examine the ideas that have "stuck" over the years—those things you've come up with and continued to use or build into businesses— you'll probably find they would have been just as exciting a week or a month after you thought of them as they were the first day.

Because a Hunter's impulsiveness and ability for instant enthusiasm can be a liability—scattering her focus—a great technique is to write down ideas as they come, but not to act on them for at least a day or three. While procrastination is defined as one of the characteristics of ADHD, that usually applies only to procrastinating over Farmer-like duties. Hunters often have the opposite problem, caused by their impulsiveness and instinct to leap into things. A psychiatrist who has ADHD himself tells the humorous story of how he proposed to a dozen different women on their first dates; fortunately none said yes. Other people leap into business decisions—particularly when it's two Hunters having the conversation—and make instant decisions that, on reflection, turn out to be ill-advised.

Similarly the urge to quit and move on is often very strong in Hunters, at least the first few times it hits. Several ADHD adults I've spoken with have told about going through ten, fifteen, and—in one case—over thirty jobs before they realized that they could resist that impulse to move on when it first struck. Sticking with the job for just another day, much the way AA advises alcoholics to stay sober "one day at a time," leads eventually to a point where staying with the job is more comfortable than the thought of leaving it. (This same strategy works well when applied to relationships.)

Even though psychiatrists tell us that Hunters are notorious procrastinators, "intentional procrastination" is a skill we still must cultivate. Set your idea aside and examine it again in a few days or a week, when the light and the mood are different, and see if it still sparkles as brilliantly. If it does, then put together a clear and cogent (and written) plan to accomplish it, with specific milestones and points to hand off to others, so it doesn't end up another "many started, few finished" project.

Picking Out the Prey
What's Your Best Business Goal?

*Nothing contributes so much to tranquilize the mind as
a steady purpose—a point on which the soul may fix its
intellectual eye.*

MARY SHELLEY, Frankenstein

Finding Your Purpose

Before we head out into the world, we must have an idea about the
goal of our hunt. Many people believe that their goal is only to build
a successful business in a particular industry, or only to feed their
family.

But there's something that must come before setting goals: purpose. Purpose is your personal destiny. It's the reason you're on this
Earth. For each of us it's different and very real. Intuitively we all
know what our purpose is. The challenge is to bring that intuition to
consciousness.

If we set goals for ourselves that are not consistent with the purpose
of our lives, then we'll find ourselves constantly frustrated, running up

against the proverbial brick wall. We'll not succeed, or if we do, it will be a hollow victory. Life will seem dry and empty, and even the hunt toward the goal will become boring in a short time.

On the other hand, when our goals are based on an understanding of our purpose, then achievement of them flows down like water from the mountains. Universal forces that forge human destiny and propel us through life, as real and as invisible as gravity, will draw us to our goals and produce success in our endeavors.

Overlaid on all of this is the issue of ADHD. For many Hunter adults in the business world, just keeping a job or relationship intact has been such an exhausting task that they haven't had time to consider such issues as purpose and goals. Now is the time.

So the first challenge to be successful in business is to discover something very personal—your purpose.

What Has Always Been Fun for You?

One of the first clues to discovering your purpose is to look back over your life and remember those things that have given you the greatest satisfaction. By this, I'm not referring to those moments of "greatest fun," the best sex or greatest party or most exciting movie. It's something much deeper and more subtle than that.

Psychologists have long known that humans have a "hierarchy of needs," often characterized as a pyramid and attributed to Abraham Maslow. At the lower levels of this pyramid are the needs for food, shelter, companionship, and security. They're our basic needs and the first ones that we'll struggle for. Higher up come social needs, status, power, pleasure, the things that we'll attend to once our first needs are secured. And at the top of the pyramid is self-actualization, the thing that few people ever really even understand, much less intentionally try to achieve.

This self-actualization is a fundamental spiritual need, the highest aspiration of all humans—be they religious or atheist. It's as deep and healing as standing on the edge of the Grand Canyon and looking out in wonder; when you stand under a starry sky and feel the magnificence of creation; or walking through a forest and sensing the life flowing through the trees, the plants, and the hidden animals.

For each of us, our ability to touch our own self-actualization is different. When we discover it, it becomes the core of our purpose.

So after you finish the next few paragraphs, put this book down, close your eyes in a quiet place, and ask yourself:

What have my most fulfilling moments been?

How have I visualized myself in my most secret fantasies?

What have I done in my life that has given me the greatest—and most lasting—pleasure?

Who are my heroes, and how do they seem heroic to me because my purpose is similar to theirs?

From the answers to these questions should come a sense of your purpose. It may not be definable immediately; it may be days before you can even articulate it in words. But when you get close to it, you'll intuitively know it. And then you can set your true goals.

Here's one final clue: the purpose of every person is connected, in some way, with the assistance of others.

Most people have heard the old Boy Scout oath to "do a good deed daily." What most don't know is the original Boy Scout definition of a good deed: it is something that helps another person but in such a way that they don't know it was you who helped them.

When you create or participate in a business that fills other people's needs on one level or another, and run or work in that business with an eye to serving both your customers and employees, it is the best first step to creating a powerful and lasting company. The scam artists and get-rich-quick people are doomed to a life of discontent, and their businesses are always at risk.

Setting Business Goals . . .
and Reaching Them

Once you've come to some sense of your purpose, then look at the world of opportunity to select or create a goal. The goal should be something tangible and definable, one you can visualize yourself achieving, and one consistent with your Hunter characteristics. Both through the process of achieving it, and through its actual attainment, you'll intuitively know that you're fulfilling your purpose. (Just as you'll know that you're not fulfilling your purpose if you hate getting up every morning to go to work.)

In the business world there are generally two ways to start something new and entrepreneurial. The first, and the hardest, is to create something altogether new. Edison's building the first electric power-generating station in New York or his creation of the phonograph, for example. This is the realm of the true inventor, the ultimate Hunter.

The second method is to take an existing idea and improve on it. When Henry Ford started making the Model A, he wasn't the first person to build a car. His wasn't even the first car company. He was, however, the first person to improve on the manufacturing process by using an assembly line, so cars could be inexpensively mass produced.

Similarly, when traveling milkshake-mixer salesman Ray Kroc founded McDonalds, he wasn't the first to market burgers. In fact, there were dozens, perhaps hundreds of fast-food hamburger places across the country, many started by other people under different names with the help of the original McDonald brothers. What Kroc did that was different was to bring absolute consistency and predictability, and the highest technologically possible quality, to the product. If a burger sat for more than ten minutes, it was not to be sold, but to be thrown out. This was unheard of among the proprietors of burger stands—but beloved by millions of Americans.

How to Find New Opportunities

There's an old joke in the advertising business that says: When you steal another person's idea in literature, that's called plagiarism, and they'll throw you in jail. When you steal another person's idea in advertising or business, it's called "applying proven marketing principles," and they give you a raise and a promotion.

It's really true that there's very little new under the sun. But there are so many, many ways that products or services that are being offered now can be manufactured or produced or marketed better.

So the first step is to (metaphorically) get out your binoculars and start examining the marketplace. What kinds of businesses are interesting to you? What would be fun to do? What have you historically been good at? What might hold your interest for a few years?

Then, having narrowed that down to a few broad categories among those existing businesses, where are there market opportunities? How might what somebody else is doing be done better?

For example, in 1983 Louise and I moved from New Hampshire to Atlanta. I'd just spent a year working as a freelance writer, after building up the New England Salem Children's Village in New Hampshire and turning it over to a brilliant and capable Farmer. An old friend in New York and I were starting the electronics mail-order company I mentioned earlier, and I needed to fly to New York every month to meet with him.

After going through three travel agencies in the area and finding all of them unsatisfying, I knew that there was an opportunity in suburban Atlanta to build a good travel agency business. All the agents I dealt with had a frustratingly bureaucratic mentality, having worked in a regulated industry. Interestingly enough, just that year the travel agency industry was being deregulated.

So Louise and I began our scouting, along with a friend from New Hampshire who owned one of that state's most innovative travel agencies. We traveled around the city "shopping" travel agencies, looking for companies that were actually successful. We subscribed to the industry publications and read about agencies doing innovative things in other cities. We also took several trips around the country and "shopped" travel agencies in other cities that were doing well.

In many of those agencies, we told the owners up front that we were from Atlanta, would never represent any competition to them, and asked if we could buy them lunch and pick their brains. I was amazed at how many of these entrepreneurs said an enthusiastic "yes," and then shared the most intimate details of their businesses with us. From that—and similar annual pilgrimages with another friend in Atlanta who owns a travel agency on the other side of town—the three of us (Louise, our friend from New Hampshire, and me) started International Wholesale Travel, and then the retail Sprayberry Travel.

We applied old ideas from the airlines to build our travel agency. We had a frequent flyer program, for example, that was administered through our agency; a secretaries club, with regular free luncheons sponsored by the airlines; and cruise nights with movies and wine-tasting parties. By these tactics, and defining as our niche the small- to medium-sized companies that were ignored by the mega-travel-agencies and poorly served by the mom-and-pop shops, we built the company up to $5 million in annual sales when we sold it in 1986 to move to Europe. (The business was doing over $20 million a few years later.) We'd also made the front page of the *Wall Street Journal* as one of the innovators of the travel industry, and I'd spoken at dozens of travel industry conferences and functions around the country, eventually being sponsored by KLM Airlines and American Express to train travel agents at annual conferences in Amsterdam.

My point isn't to brag about this accomplishment. It's to show that we didn't do anything "new," but applied "proven marketing principles" in a new way to an old industry. We simply did our homework, and then created a business that was something we thought would be fun and congruent with our goals at that time (our kids have now seen the world several times over).

We also segmented out the work along Hunter-Farmer lines, with me creating the new marketing programs, designing literature, and making sales calls, while Louise managed the company on a day-to-day basis and supervised the reservations staff.

You can do the same, be it with ice cream, printing, or steel.

Do People Really Want It?

I've been astounded, over the years, by the number of "million-dollar ideas" people have come to me with—for products that they themselves wouldn't buy. "The average person would love this," they'll say, "although I don't really need one."

Examine your idea in the hard light of reality. Try preselling it to a few people and get their reactions. In the world of direct mail, it's not at all unusual to do a "test mailing" offering a new product or service to only a few thousand people and, if the response is very poor, to cut the losses by simply refunding people's money in a timely fashion with an apology.

Is It Franchisable?

If you're going to follow the earlier dictum of creating a business and a business plan that could be franchised, then this is the first question you should ask yourself when you define an entrepreneurial goal. Is this something that any person with a bit of enthusiasm and pluck and average intelligence could do?

If the answer is no, or you're considering something like becoming a consultant, that's not necessarily a bad choice. Just realize up front that you're creating a job for yourself, not a business. And when you leave, or if you were to become disabled or disinterested, the equity in that would probably be close to nil.

A franchisable or salable business, on the other hand, both produces income for you (at least over the long term) and also builds equity. It's something that you can sell, a savings account of sorts. And if you orga-nize it from the beginning in this franchise model, then you'll find it quite easy to sell, even if it's not the sort of thing that you'd want to franchise.

Decide on the Appropriate Company Structure

Your options for creating an organization are many. These include part-nerships, corporations, sole proprietorships, purchasing franchises from others, purchasing the license to use another's name or product, and professional corporations.

I broke my back skydiving in 1970, and that led to the failure of my first real business, a TV and electronics repair shop that I started and ran while attending college. I was nineteen years old and didn't really know much about business. I had five employees and a debt of about $9,000 that I couldn't pay. Unfortunately I hadn't incorporated (like so many Hunters in their early business years, it seemed to me to be too much trouble), so when I took the (bad) advice of an attorney and declared bankruptcy, it devastated my personal credit for the next seven years. Over the following three years, I built up another business to national status and paid back the full $9,000 in debt, even the $3,000 that the bank had already written off (they weren't altogether sure how to book my repayment—although they took the money!). All this didn't matter a whit to my credit rating. Even though by 1975 I was earning more than the president of my bank, and I'd paid back my bankruptcy in full, the bank still wouldn't issue me a credit card.

Ever since then—even though I've not since had a business col-lapse to the point of bankruptcy (I've sold a few and closed a few)—I've always incorporated. A *corporation,* for legal purposes, is essentially a new entity, a new "person." So, if the corporation doesn't fare well, it may not reflect poorly on you personally. And it's much easier to sell the stock or assets of a corporation, as they're always kept separate from your own personal assets.

In most states it costs about $300 and you can do it yourself. The forms are often available online. The people with your state government's office will be glad to walk you through filling out a few simple forms, and take their fees. If you have a few more dollars and not as much time, you can hire an attorney to do it for you. There are also online vendors that will incorporate you in any of the fifty states for a very modest fee. (I used a company that was on the CompuServe Mall several times.)

So step one is to incorporate.

Step two is to be very wary about partnerships, unless some very specific conditions apply.

Unincorporated partnerships are a legal morass, as you're taking personal responsibility not only for yourself but also for the actions of your partners. I have a good friend who, as I write these words, is trying to figure out how to pay off the $40,000 that his partner borrowed and then walked off with in the partnership's name, leaving my friend personally responsible for the debt.

But even incorporated partnerships can be a mess. When working as a business consultant over the years, nearly every company I've encountered that was in dire straits was in trouble because the partners—who'd always started out as the best of friends—had become the worst of enemies.

A friend and business mentor once made the wry observation that a partnership contains all the worst parts of marriage (arguments over how to do things, who does what, how the money is spent, what belongs to whom) and doesn't even include sex!

If you must take in a partner for either money or expertise, take her in as a minority stockholder (less than 50 percent), and on the front end, write a buy-sell agreement that if either party wants out, the other has first option to buy her stock. Whatever price the selling party puts on the stock also has to be the price that she'd be willing to finance and pay for the other party's stock, so fairness is always guaranteed.

The one exception to this warning about partnerships is when people bring widely disparate skills, talents, and personalities to the partnership. A Hunter-Farmer partnership can be a good start, but there also must be a clear definition of who's going to do what—who has responsibility and authority in what specific areas of the business. Without these clear definitions disaster is predictable, as each party meddles in the responsibilities of the other. With these definitions it's possible to have a working arrangement that benefits both partners and helps build a vital business. But even then the company's structure should be a corporation, with the partners owning equal amounts of stock.

Franchises

Purchasing franchises or buying licenses can be problematic. There are some excellent franchise companies in the world, but depending on the franchise it can be difficult to be entrepreneurial in the context of a franchise. You have to dance to the tune of the franchiser, and are wed to him for the life of the contract. The people for whom it's often most suitable to purchase a franchise are those who want to own their own business with little risk and can see themselves doing the same thing, making an average wage, for the next thirty years. Also, it's for those who purchase the franchise as an investment and plan to hire competent management. (Many owners of the larger franchises, such as McDonald's, fall into this camp.) Neither are Hunter entrepreneurs, as defined in this book.

On the other hand, there are many franchises where Hunters can shine. The franchise provides the external structure necessary, and the business is such that there's constant variety to keep the Hunter engaged. These include printing, travel, consulting, and many sales-driven franchises. Regardless of the industry or franchise, though, check out the corporate culture of the franchiser to see if he encourages or discourages innovation and change. If the former, it may be right for you: if the latter, beware.

Husband-Wife Teams in Business

Many people start businesses with their spouses. This can be particularly difficult, as having a successful marriage is not easy in itself, and the added strains of running a business together can rip people apart. On the other hand, if the husband and wife respect each other, have a strong friendship, and keep in mind some important rules unique to married business partners, they may find that the company provides them with both a source of income and an opportunity to spend time together.

Over the years I've known dozens of husband-wife business teams, and most are Hunter-Farmer couples. One couple owns a successful travel agency, and it provides them with the tax-deductible opportunity to travel the world. Another couple runs a consulting company: he's the consultant, and she books his time and manages the money. Virtually everybody knows or has known a married couple in business together.

However, the corporate landscape is also littered with the remnants of once-solid marriages torn apart by business. Sometimes it leads to divorce, although more often I've seen couples simply drift apart, separated by the wall of years of anger and resentment caused by different business styles or business disagreements.

If you're considering going into business with your husband or wife, consider the following pointers.

1. Don't use ADHD as an excuse to dump responsibility onto the spouse, or else realize that it's probably inevitable and plan for it. The partner who's the starting force in the business is most often the Hunter. This person gets things going, moving along at a quick pace . . . and then sometimes loses interest. The spouse finds himself having to hold together the pieces of the first project while the Hunter is off onto something else. This leaves the dumped-on spouse feeling resentful: "You're always running off, doing the fun stuff, and I'm left here stuck with the details."

One solution, if the marriage is a Hunter-Farmer one, is to decide from the beginning that this is the course the business relationship will probably take and plan for it. If the business is intrinsically high stimulation, such as consulting, then it may be appropriate for one person to be the outside person and the other staff the inside. The high level of change in the business will keep the Hunter occupied and interested, and the Farmer will keep the checkbook balanced and the bills paid. But if the business is a rather day-to-day venture, the risk is that the Hunter spouse may end up going off in some altogether different direction from what was first envisaged, functionally doubling the work for the Farmer. This is rarely constructive.

The solution is to realize up front that the Hunter partner probably won't be there for the long term. As discussed earlier in this book, the Hunter partner ends up as a consultant to the business, or transfers control of it altogether to the Farmer spouse.

Where this often breaks down is when the Hunter is unwilling to relinquish control to the Farmer, yet also refuses to be responsible for the details. Knowledge of ADHD can even become an excuse for such behavior, adding to the stresses in the business and marriage relationship.

Planning for this in advance—discussing it openly, and developing plans to deal with the inevitable loss of interest that the Hunter will experience—can help prevent this type of problem. There also should be a partnership agreement between the spouses that commits the Hunter to a process that will prevent the Farmer from burning out.

2. Don't take problems home or to bed. There's an old rule of marriage that says, "Don't ever go to bed angry." The corollary for spouses in business together is: "Don't take work home with you." Spouse-partners who are successful in both their business and marriage are usually acutely aware of this rule. They don't discuss business at home, and particularly never discuss it in bed. At the office they plan time to meet every day or every week, so that the cares and problems of the office don't end up being served over dessert at home.

Another aspect of this is the importance of not taking issues of the marriage into the workplace. Job applicants will sometimes shy away from working for a married couple, because there's often a grain of truth to stories of the mom-and-pop shop where mom and pop are always fighting.

While there's something almost romantic about the notion of being such total partners that a couple is both in business and married, it's important to remember that the business partnership and the marriage are separate entities. Each requires its own special time, care, and consideration. By splitting off work time from personal time, it's much more likely that the marriage won't be destroyed by the business or that the problems of marriage won't be dragged into the office.

If you're the ADHD partner in the business-marriage, it's easy to jump in and blurt out things that may not be well thought out. In a purely business relationship, there's a larger margin for error: you can hire new employees or find a new job. In a business-marriage, though, this can be disaster. A good solution is to write down the issues you intend to discuss, and confine discussions of business to specific prearranged meeting times.

3. Respect the opinions and value the work of each other. Wives or husbands are not slave labor, although I've known more than one couple in business together where it appeared that this was the belief of the (usually ADHD) spouse. Such perspectives are not only destructive to the business, but to the marriage as well.

Just as in a normal business partnership, a business relationship between spouses will only work if both parties have a healthy respect for the abilities and opinions of the other. If you don't value your spouse's business abilities and opinions as highly as you do your own, don't go into business together.

4. Define areas of responsibility. This is perhaps the most important and problematic area of business between spouses. Issues such as who controls the money, who makes what decisions, and who ultimately runs the business are intrinsically related to power within the relationship. The nature of interpersonal power and how it's used between people is one of the most common problems in marriage.

So it's important, from the outset, to define who has what responsibilities and what powers, and to consider this in the context of the different Hunter and Farmer abilities people may bring to the relationship.

For example, in one partnership I know of, the husband cannot spend more than $100 of company money without the wife's approval. He's an impulsive Hunter, and she's the detail person in the partnership, and so logically is responsible for the finances. With that responsibility must come authority.

Who hires and fires? Who controls the money? Who initiates or approves new programs and plans?

While it sounds romantic to say that all these types of issues will be dealt with as partners, with each person having equal say, in reality it rarely works. Before you begin the business, make a list of the jobs in the company and split them up. Always correlate authority with responsibility, and be realistic about matching jobs with skills and personality types, keeping in mind the inevitable challenges that the ADHD partner will confront.

It is possible to have a successful business partnership between spouses, as thousands of couples have demonstrated. If these simple rules aren't followed, however, what started out as a fun business and marriage may end up with divorce in both arenas.

Hunting for Success

Building a Life With, Through, and in Spite of Your ADHD

10

Preparing for the Hunt
Ways to Push Through ADHD

Self-reverence, self-knowledge, self-control,
These three alone lead life to sovereign power.
ALFRED, LORD TENNYSON, *OENONE*

Regardless of the business role you've chosen for your life, there are certain strategies that will make use of your inherent strengths and bring success to your endeavors. Because Hunters sense time differently than Farmers, and because they have a different view of themselves and the world, these strategies are uniquely powerful for Hunters in the business realm.

When Native Americans who lived in the plains would prepare for a major hunting expedition, they'd go through elaborate rituals: dancing and prayer, singing and chanting, wearing masks and paint. All served to build in them a sense that they were in harmony with their purpose, and to focus their minds on the single point of the hunt ahead.

In modern society many successful people have found that there is a similar set of rituals we can do to overcome our fears, reprogram our minds, and prepare for success in business. Whether we are looking for a job, tracking down a new customer, or taking on an opponent in court, the rituals apply.

Overcoming Negative Self-Talk

When we sit down and listen to other people tell us about themselves and their lives, we discover that they have a lot of stories they tell themselves about how things are and why they are that way. They know that they can't become rich because their parents weren't or that only dishonest people can become successful in business. They can't lose weight because food is the substitute for the love they never felt from their parents. They've had a hard time with relationships ever since that first love jilted them. They can't do cold-calling in sales because they can't stand rejection. On and on these sad stories go, and if you draw them out from people, they'll ramble on for hours.

These stories, which we accumulate along the course of our lives, are the lens through which we view reality. They color our perception of the world around us, our place in it, what other people are like, and of what we can and cannot do. These stories come from our parents, our peers, books we read, movies we've seen, and people we've heard on *Donahue*. And they can either build us up or tear us down.

For people with ADHD there's often a huge storehouse of such stories, and they can be particularly destructive in adult life. As children, regardless of how bright we are, Hunters often have difficulty in school because of the boring demands of homework or the structure of the classroom that demands continual focused concentration. In later life there's the guilt associated with all those projects that were started but never finished; the feelings of missed potential; and the persistent, awful feeling that we know we should be able to do better, but just can't seem to pull it off over the long term.

So step one in our strategy is to examine our own stories—the things we tell ourselves about why we are the way we are, and the ideas we have about how the world works. And realize, here and now as you're reading these words, that they are just stories. They may or may not be true. And you have the power to change them if you want to.

Stand Up Straight

The famous psychologist William James observed that most people think behavior follows feelings. If a person walks around slouching with a frown, it's probably because he's depressed at that moment, or worried. While this is true, James says, the reciprocal is also true, but most people are totally unaware of it. When feeling down, if you dress well, stand up straight, hold your chin and chest high, and—as the British say—"keep a stiff upper lip," James tells us that we'll actually change our feelings!

Look back over your life and you can probably remember specific situations when this was true for you. That first time you wore a suit or gown at the senior prom—or when you took a friend for a drive in your first new car. By changing our circumstances, over which we do have control, we can actually change our emotions, over which most people think they have no control.

For someone battered by a lifetime of ADHD-caused failures, this may seem difficult. But it works.

You Can't Think about Two Things at the Same Time

John Roy is a therapist in Maine who shared with me one of his most powerful techniques for dealing with depressed or defeatist ADHD patients. He points out to them that it's a physical and psychological impossibility to think about two things at the same time.

They come into his office or his groups full of sad thoughts, wanting to tell their sad stories, full of complaints and anger and bitterness, the history of all their failures. And John will get them to shift the conversation to things they're interested in, they hope for, they care about—and watch them change.

One time John walked into the hospital room of a patient of his who was crumpled up on the edge of his bed, sobbing in agony. John put his hand on the man's shoulder and, instead of saying (as the man expected), "What's wrong, you poor fellow?" John said instead, "What was the happiest time of your life?"

The fellow sat up with a startled look and began to think; he then told John a long story about this wonderful vacation he'd taken years earlier with his family. As he told the story, he became more and more animated, discovering that, even in the midst of his "nervous break-down," he could feel positive emotions. It was the beginning of his recovery.

This isn't feel-good psychobabble or new age psychology. It's a func-tional truth: the conscious mind can only hold one thought at a time. And—startlingly enough—you control, to an extent you probably never dreamed possible, what those thoughts are and will be.

For Hunters one of the most common stories is: "I have a men-tal disorder, a neurological imbalance in my brain, and therefore I'm doomed to forever be a wreck." Some people are so attached to their ADHD illness, to their sense of themselves as a victim, that they even resist the idea that being a Hunter may have its positive sides. They'd rather put their life in the hands of others, blame their fail-ures on their genes, and embark on a never-ending quest for the "best medication."

While modern psychiatry and psychology does much good, and bringing the concept of ADHD to people is often liberating and enlightening, explaining much about their lives, this unfortunate sub-set of Hunters are so attached to being ill that nothing short of a bomb blast will move them off-center. They become dependent on their thera-pists and medications, and paralyzed by the thought of making inde-pendent decisions. (Such people, however, probably would not have read this far into this book.)

Hamid Bey, one of my early mentors, told me, "What a man thinks about he can become. What he persistently thinks about, he cannot help but become." It's a two-edged sword, however. In our unfortunate age of TV-talk-show psychology and ever-new fads of "how to be a victim of your past," most people are unaware that they're using this power to defeat, rather than to repair or empower, themselves.

So examine your stories, particularly those about what you can and cannot do because of ADHD, and realize that you may be able to change them.

Accept the Worst, and Then Make It Better

Hunters, feeling a constant sense of impending doom, often spend much of their lives fearing the worst. But how about accepting the worst, and then moving on, releasing the fear?

My wife, a consummate Farmer with extraordinary common sense, has followed me around the world several times, through many businesses, and watched us build and spend several small fortunes (or, at least, what seemed to us to be fortunes). My business and other types of Hunter risk-taking might drive other spouses to divorce (it was on one of our first dates that I broke my back skydiving). But Louise has developed a great technique for dealing with her fears of the future and the unknown.

"I always ask myself, 'What's the worst that can happen?'" she says. "And when I look at that, and accept it, then anything that does happen different is a great improvement. It's a liberating feeling to know that even the worst isn't the end, that we can always just pick up and proceed."

In starting a new business venture, it's also often useful to have a fallback position. These could range from a large savings account to a second job to the promise of a job if your venture doesn't work out.

There are two schools of thought on this. One school says that if you have a fallback, you won't be forced or motivated to give it your all; the other says that if you have a fallback, at least you won't be confronting disaster if your business fails. I believe that the best fallback is to know that you'll always be able to pick yourself up, dust yourself off, and carry on. It's the skills of living and doing that breed this kind of confidence. But I'm also not opposed to putting a little money in the bank for a rainy day (although, frankly, I rarely have done so).

Because Hunters often have a lifetime of unfinished projects behind them, of unfulfilled potentials, it may be that not having the fallback position creates just the edge that we need to keep us on course, even through the boring times.

Feelings Are Your Connection to Intuitive Knowledge

We are all connected in some extraordinary fashion to a universal and intuitive knowledge of life. Whether you take a Jungian view or a religious perspective or just call it accumulated wisdom or racial memory, a part of us knows what's right and what's wrong for us. This is different from the stories we tell ourselves, which I mentioned earlier. It's more subtle. This wisdom is in our feelings, below the level of our thoughts.

Learning to listen to our feelings is something very new, and often odd, for people in Western civilization (and particularly for men). Rationality, the mechanical universe, and the notion that thought is supreme have come to be basic assumptions for many people. Yet our feelings are our guides to our intuition, which can be our greatest power.

I'm not talking here about needing to yell about your parents, or crying or scream therapy, but rather a very simple concept. When you find yourself reacting emotionally to a business idea, examine that emotion and see if it's founded in some intuitive truth.

This is of particular importance to Hunters because of the emotional baggage we carry from childhood—which may obscure at times our access to our real feelings—and our frequent desire for high stimulation. This self-knowledge, however, lets us begin the process of sorting through the jumble of stuff going on inside our minds and hearts, and access true intuitional wisdom.

Learning the Difference between Intuition and Fear

Some people have fear as one of the dominating forces in their lives. They're afraid of relationships, afraid to start businesses, afraid to take a new job, afraid of the unknown.

For Hunters this is a particular issue because most have lived with a lifetime of feeling that doom is just over their shoulder. While this may have helped our ancestors survive from predators in the jungle or forest, it can be a terrible distraction in the modern world.

Fear is not an intuitive feeling: it's counterintuitive. Fear is almost always the result of destructive self-talk, and is most effectively overcome through confrontation.

Fear of failure is the most debilitating of all fears in business, and it can be paralyzing. Remind yourself that in the very same year that Babe Ruth hit more home runs than any other man in the history of baseball, he also struck out more times than any other player. Fear of failure is conquered by perseverance and by recognizing that failure is a normal part of life and a requisite for learning.

A speaker I heard years ago told a story about a young man who came to the chairman of a large corporation and said, "Sir, I want to end up with your job when you retire. How can I do that?"

The old man lifted one eyebrow, thought for a moment, removed his cigar from his mouth, and said, "Don't make any mistakes."

"But, sir, how can I not make mistakes?" the young man asked.

The chairman pointed at him with the cigar and said, "Get experience."

"And how do I do that, sir?" the young man said.

At which point the chairman leaned back in his chair, returned the cigar to his mouth, smiled, and said in a gruff voice, "Make a lot of mistakes. And learn from them."

Overcoming Forgetfulness:
Learn Original Awareness

The first step in learning to remember things is to learn to pay attention in the first place. This is a particular challenge for Hunters, whose minds are often zooming in a hundred directions. When it comes time to find the car keys, they seem to have been swallowed by a denizen of the twilight zone. Combs and brushes disappear with frightening regularity—and it's particularly distressing when a wallet or purse is constantly misplaced.

The solution for this is to learn the concept of original awareness. As you set down the car keys, look for a moment at the top of the kitchen counter where you're putting them, and take notice of them there. When people can't remember things, it's most often because they failed to pay attention to them in the first place.

This sounds self-evident, but it's really a powerful technique for Hunters (or anyone else). If your attention wanders in a meeting and you feel you might "misplace" an idea or topic, ask for it to be repeated. Generally, instead of being offended, people are flattered that you consider what they're saying important enough that you'd want them to repeat it. And, if you're running a business meeting, write up an agenda for the meeting; when you see yourself or others wandering afield, gently bring them (or yourself) back on track.

Similarly, when introduced to someone new, most people are so busy thinking about what they're going to say, or worrying about the impression they may make, that they don't "hear" the other person's name in the first place. Instead try simply repeating the other person's name back to him: "I'm pleased to meet you, Mr. Jones," and then look for an opportunity to use his name in the next few sentences again. It makes him feel good but, more important, it creates original awareness.

This ability to both remember things and events and to remember people's names, is critical to success in business. Few things offend a prospective client more than having his name forgotten. Similarly enormous amounts of time are wasted, which could have been put to more productive use, because the Hunter is constantly searching for things that didn't have to be lost in the first place.

Memorize Lists with Absurd Visualizations

Because one of the characteristics of ADHD is "difficulty with auditory processing," Hunters tend to be visual thinkers, and often have difficulty remembering words, which can be a real liability in business. They'll forget something while simply walking from one room to the next, if it's based on words. Sometimes it's a challenge just "staying with the topic" in a business meeting.

The flip side of this is that Hunters are great visual processors, and so you can use the simple technique of creating pictures in your mind to represent concepts or things you want to remember. Ordinary pictures are easily forgotten, however: it's absurd pictures that have the greatest memorability. If you wanted to memorize a list of things to do, for example, simply convert each item on the list to an absurd picture.

Go to the store and buy bread is visualized as driving with John Dillinger to the store, running in, machine guns blazing, and running out with a pile of bread as high as your chin. Make the bank deposit becomes a mental image of pouring a huge deposit into the depository slot in the bank. Drop by the dry cleaners and pick up the shirts is visualized as hundreds of empty starched shirts marching down the street like something out of the twilight zone. And pick up cough medicine at the drug store for your child turns into a mental picture of standing in front of the drugstore and sneezing so hard that the store blows over.

Do you see the pictures? Visualize them in your mind.

Now, let's create a list from these pictures, so we know that we've done them all. Let's connect them. Visualize that the stuffed depository slot at the bank is overfilled with the bread from the store you just robbed. Then visualize the marching shirts parading away from the bank, fleeing a Pillsbury Doughboy monster you've created there, á la

Ghostbusters, by putting the bread into the depository. Now visualize the shirts running by you, each reaching out to tickle your nose until you sneeze so powerfully that it blows over the drug store.

Now you have memorized a list—and could repeat it forward, backward, or in either direction from the middle. If you actually visualized these things, you'll probably even remember this list weeks or months from now, effortlessly. And the list could just as easily have been ten or twenty things as four!

This ability to remember names and to quickly memorize lists of things, be they To Do's or lists of products, can be a very powerful tool in business. And learning these simple exercises is a great way around the common ADHD problem/characteristic of "not paying attention" and therefore not remembering details.

Nutrition and Health: Plan Your Diet

Most of the Hunter businesspeople I've talked with over the years are sugar junkies: there's some speculation this may have to do with a Hunter's need to be able to draw on huge stores of energy for a short time in the midst of a hunt. The result is a "hair trigger" sugar metabolism, which alternately craves and then is overwhelmed by (and even gets a bit of a high from) sweets.

Many Hunters are overly fond of alcohol, which may be related to how easily bored Hunters are. With their elastic time-sense, unless they're doing something, on the Hunt, time seems to slow down, and alcohol changes that sense of boring slow-time to something more tolerable. But the downside of drinking in a business context is obvious.

Junk food is often a staple for busy Hunter businesspeople. Who wants to take the time to prepare and eat a proper meal, particularly when there's exciting work to be done?

It was popular a few years ago to describe many of these ADHD characteristics, particularly in men, as a "Type A" personality, and correlations were made between this type of personality and heart disease or other problems. The concept of adult ADHD is too recent for there to have been any studies on "normal" adult ADHD populations. One study, however, was done recently with adults who were diagnosed as ADHD in childhood (meaning that they were more likely to have started out as "problem children," which motivated somebody to seek a diagnosis). Even though the population sample starts out skewed and the results must be seen in this light, this study showed that they tend to live shorter lives than non-ADHD adults.*

Nutrition and diet must play a role in this, and obviously healthy businesspeople are more productive businesspeople.

Diet and exercise are two simple demands of the body and mind of the Hunter. To be successful in business or in life, one must first be functional. Daily exercise has been demonstrated to improve mental functioning, and may even reduce the severity of ADHD "symptoms." On the ADD Forum on CompuServe, one person told the story of attending an elementary school in Taiwan where between every class there was a ten-minute exercise period in which kids were encouraged to run around and work up a sweat. In this person's opinion, this did much to resolve "problem behavior" among the ADHD population in that school.

Many Hunters have told me that if they eat much sugar, or fail to eat several small nonsugary meals during the day, they turn unreasonably irritable and their attention span becomes even shorter. Nobody, to the best of my knowledge, has done any studies linking hypoglycemia to ADHD (pro or con), but following a rational diet and avoiding the temptation to binge on sugar is only common sense.

Read, Listen, and Keep Inspired

These techniques are some of the ways Hunters can prepare themselves for success in the business world.

---

*See "Got ADHD? You May Live a Shorter Life, Study Shows," by Susan Donaldson James, *NBC News,* February 26, 2015, http://goo.gl/Svssn3.

Certainly there are many others, and it seems that many of the success and motivation books written over the past fifty years have been largely written by, and for, Hunters. Read the biographies of so many motivational speakers and writers, and you'll see staring out at you the typical profile of an ADHD adult.

So don't be embarrassed to buy those tapes or pick up those books in the bookstore. Don't feel that only losers hook into that "motivational stuff."

It's real, and particularly real for Hunters. It works.

11

Tracking the Prey
Heading for Success

To strive, to seek, to find, and not to yield.
ALFRED, LORD TENNYSON, *ULYSSES*

Our high schools and colleges, unfortunately, do not teach strategies for success, and usually have virtually nothing to offer by way of success strategies for Hunters.

We graduate knowing which year Columbus allegedly discovered America, Newton's laws of motion, and the details of an isosceles triangle—but little about how to reshape our own will, to reorder our time, to inspire ourselves and others, or to overcome our Hunter impulsiveness. The essentials of taking charge of our lives to build and run a company are largely lost. Who among us has had a class in goal setting, leadership, time management, or how to find peace within ourselves amid the frenetic and sustained explosion of the business day?

From the first notion to begin a business or join the workplace to the final steps of managing a mature enterprise, the Hunter in the business world most often must rely on new knowledge from her own experience. Mentors are few in our modern society, and it's rare that experienced businesspeople with a clear understanding of the ADHD mindset can or will share their knowledge. So people grope their way along, very often learning from their failures before enjoying their successes.

Assuming you know the basics of balancing a checkbook and filing taxes (or finding a bookkeeper to do it for you!), here are some hard-learned tips necessary for entrepreneurial survival but absent from the classroom or textbooks.

Tips for Entrepreneurial Survival

Write Down Your Goal

Whether you've decided to start a business, get a new job, or become the next Robert Ludlum, the first step in tracking your quarry—in achieving your goal—is to write it down. Make it short and sweet: one sentence should do it, two or three words is even better. (Hunters know the importance of brevity!)

Write it on the back of a business card, and put it in your wallet in a place where whenever you open your wallet, you'll glance at it. Put one on the mirror in your bathroom. Stick a small one near the speedometer on the dash of your car, where you can see it but others in the car can't.

This begins the process of retraining your unconscious—helping you hold an image of your goal and visualize yourself achieving it. You'll be amazed after doing this how quickly ideas to help you achieve your goals will begin flowing into your mind. (Don't forget the notebook and pen!)

Organizing Your Hunt

Then develop your action plan. How are you going to reach your goal? What are your timelines? What are the individual steps to get there?

People with ADHD nearly always have the problem of being disorganized. It may be because a Hunter is visually oriented and aware of everything at once, or it may have some other basis. But it certainly can be a problem, regardless of its source.

Organizational strategies can be learned, however, and they're not particularly difficult, even for Hunters. One of the best I've come across over the years is to make a daily To Do list on a legal pad. Have two boxes on the desk labeled "A" and "B," and an empty drawer labeled "C." Everything on the list, and every piece of paper that comes into the office, is daily prioritized into either an A, a B, or a C.

A's are things that must be done immediately. After you've defined the A's, number them in the order in which they'll be done, and then stick to the list. If there are large A's that are going to take large blocks of time, or even span over days or weeks, break them into one- or two-hour pieces, and make a new one of those an A every day.

B's are the important things that you need to get to when you're finished with all the A's. Jot down the side of your legal-pad list a B beside all the B's, and put B pieces of paper into the B box. I've found it useful to note on my list the papers in the box, because for Hunters "out of sight is out of mind."

C's are things that can wait until later, whenever that is. C's that come in the mail may be interesting offers, catalogs, correspondence that you've already answered, information from competitors, and so on. The C paper gets dumped into the big empty drawer, and the C's that require action get written down on the To Do list.

Spend ten minutes every morning rewriting your list—copying things from the day before onto a new page and looking over the new day's mail. You'll find that some B's will become A's. Some will become C's. Some C's will drop off the list altogether or will begin to rise in priority. Every day look over each item and assign a letter to it.

Once a year take your "C" drawer and dump it into a box or file labeled "C Stuff from 2016," for example. You may want to create a separate file folder for correspondence, although I've found over the years that, for me, that's not so useful as to justify the effort.

This simple organizational system is the best I've ever found, and I've tried dozens. It's simple enough for the get-it-done-quickly Hunter, yet works. I've talked with many successful Hunter businesspeople, writers, and other professionals who employ this method, which was first popularized in Alan Lakein's *How to Get Control of Your Time and Life* back in the early 1970s.

Develop a Mastermind Group

Napoleon Hill was one of the early writers to tell the "secret" of the Mastermind group. In many cases this is a group of businesspeople who would get together periodically to share ideas, solve problems, and energize each other. But Hill also discussed visualizing a group of advisors in your own mind during a quiet time at home, with eyes closed, and having periodic meetings with them, each being an expert in a particular field. (It sounds odd, but really works for some people. A psychologist friend who used to do this said that he felt it was a nonthreatening way of unlocking below-consciousness knowledge.)

At the very least, develop relationships in your field, your industry, or your business community with like-minded people. Set aside the time to get together for lunch or dinner once a month, and meet with the common purpose of energizing each other. The Mastermind principle is that whenever two or more people come together for a common goal, they create a synergistic energy that is far greater than that of any two individuals working alone. It also provides an opportunity for Farmers to balance and perform reality checks for impulsive Hunters, and for Hunters to energize and inspire Farmers.

Within your company, also develop a small Mastermind group made up of those people who are your best and closest advisors. Compensate them well, and respect their opinions. Meet weekly or monthly or quarterly and review the business, its goals, and your personal goals. Discuss how the company can be used for a greater good, and develop altruistic goals as well as business goals. Consider corporate tithing.

Always Hire the Best

Andrew Carnegie, who founded U. S. Steel and died one of the richest people in America, was fond of noting that he knew nothing about the manufacture or marketing of steel. But he'd hired the best minds in the business, and he respected their opinions. That, according to him, made him successful and wealthy.

Recently one of my clients in a large corporation confided that she'd been advised by one of her peers, another person in senior management, that he would never hire somebody better than he was. "As long as you hire people who are less competent than you, your job is secure," this man had told my shocked friend.

In actual point of fact, although this conventional wisdom is all-too prevalent in corporate America, it's utter nonsense. My motto has always been to hire people better than myself in whatever area of expertise they're needed, right on up to senior management. An organization, after all, is nothing more or less than the people in it! Mediocre people will inevitably create a mediocre company.

Many Hunters, having all their lives felt somewhat "put down" by others or having experienced failure in school or early business experience, are intimidated by really competent people, particularly those who are solid Farmers. But such people are the soul of a company, and like the farmers of old who planted and nourished their crops, these modern Farmers will feed and nourish your company.

Don't Meddle, but Learn as Much as You Can

A Hunter's instinct is to mess with everything: to stick his nose into every aspect of the business and to offer opinions, whether solicited or not.

If you're going to run a successful business, you must learn to moderate this instinct.

It's good to know what and how people are doing, but most average people or good Farmers are unnerved by somebody bouncing into their workspace without warning and poking into their work. Often it makes them feel that their Hunter boss is unsure about the quality of their work, because they don't understand the Hunter's need to bounce around and continually be restimulated.

There's nothing wrong with learning every job in the place, but don't try to practice them. If you've followed the rule of hiring the best possible people, the best course of action you can take is to let them do their jobs in the way that works best for them, and give them the authority to make their own decisions.

In our newsletter business, and in an ad agency I was a partner in back in the 1970s, we'd sometimes run across "problem clients." Nine times out of ten, the situation was that a good Farmer was responsible for the advertising or the newsletter, but the company owner or the supervisor was a hyperactive Hunter who couldn't keep from meddling, always wanted changes, and always waited to the last minute to specify what the changes should be. The employee was frustrated, we were frustrated, and the Hunter employer was unintentionally sabotaging the entire process.

I've seen this in dozens of companies that have grown to the size where they need an ad agency—which is also usually the size where they need good Farmer management—and the Hunter entrepreneur who started the place is still in charge. It's a pain in the neck for both the employees of the companies and the vendors to them.

Hire a Good Farmer as a Manager

This brings us to the importance of finding a good manager, somebody to act as a flywheel to keep your Hunter instincts under control. Just as Hunters are only a small percentage of the population, so too there's a limited supply of these good Farmers who are skilled at working with people, love to attend to the details, enjoy planning, and actually look forward to follow-through.

Once the entrepreneurial phase of the company is over, it's often wise even to make this Farmer your manager, at least in certain areas. Give her control over the budget and the money, for example, so if you want to go zooming off in some new direction, you have to make a very good case for it, and she can still veto it. An empowered Farmer can build a strong and stable business. If you only give her partial authority, though, a disempowered Farmer will become so frustrated that your best efforts won't be enough to keep the person with you.

Monitor the Marketplace

One of your jobs as the company's Hunter is to keep a wary eye out. Shop the competition. Look for new ways of doing things. Travel around the country and build a small network of similar people in your same industry with whom you don't compete, so you can share ideas and techniques. Attend trade shows and seminars: learn and bring new ideas into the company.

In a competitive business this monitoring of the marketplace and the competition should be at least a monthly one-day project. In an area where you have no competition (hard to imagine, but there are some), the time is best spent brainstorming new ways to improve the product or service and talking with others around the country who run the same type of business as yours.

How to Pace Yourself

One of Hallowell and Ratey's psychiatric criteria for diagnosing ADHD is that the person starts lots of projects that he doesn't finish. This is sometimes because interest in the project wanes, particularly among children, but for Hunters in the business world it's more often because they overcommit.

Time, to a Hunter, seems like such a variable commodity. She always thinks that there'll always be a little more that she can pull out of the hat. Sure, I'll take on that responsibility; it won't take more than an hour or two, will it?

This is one of the Hunter's big traps.

One successful Hunter businessman told me: "Whenever I look at a job or project, I estimate how long it's going to take—by gut instinct. Then I stop myself and make the effort to double that time, because

I've found, over the years, that things always take twice as long as I think they're going to."

Force Yourself to Train Properly

"Force yourself" sounds like strong language, but that's what it usually takes to get an entrepreneur to invest the time and effort necessary to truly train someone to do a new job. One of the biggest stumbling blocks to growth and delegation, and one of the main reasons why employees fail and resent their bosses, is a lack of proper training.

It's incredibly frustrating to spend an hour teaching somebody how to do something that you know you can do in ten minutes. The instinct is to just do it, get it done now, and then hope that the employee either watched you and picked up all the details, or knows how to read the book or manual on how to do what you just did.

But it's a lousy trade-off.

The hours you invest in teaching people to properly do the jobs you intend to delegate to them will be returned to you in hundreds of hours of future freedom from those jobs. Street-smart businesspeople know the math of this equation, and even though it's frustrating, boring, and difficult, they force themselves to train people properly for their jobs.

Break Big Jobs into Little Pieces

I put off writing my first book (a sci-fi novel that'll never see the light of day, but a lifetime goal in any case) for thirty years. I always told myself that I was going to write it, but never could get started. It was just too big a project; the very thought of it overwhelmed me. I always figured that "someday" I'd take six months off, rent a villa on the Mediterranean, and get that book written.

"Somedays" never come, of course.

Then, in 1980, I was visiting the apartment of a friend who's a successful novelist and an ADHD Hunter. He was preparing to send off a manuscript to his publisher, and told me that the way he wrote was to do only five pages a day: no more and no less. At that rate, he told me, he'd produce several novels a year, and—before he became successful—he still had time for his "day job," which had included everything from being a spy (for our side) to a taxi driver. Now that he was making a good living from his writing, he still kept the same pace, and used the extra time for "fun and recharging."

It sounded like a good idea, and I started using it. Since then I've written nine novels, several nonfiction books, and hundreds of published magazine articles.

I've learned to apply this same principle to business projects. If we need to put together a slide presentation as a sales tool for our company, I'll allocate an hour a day to work on it. If I try to spend more time, it becomes so tedious I start procrastinating, or else the quality of my work suffers.

So, in all cases, break big projects into little pieces, and they will get done . . . even though, as a Hunter, you may have a hard time imagining it happening.

Learn to Say No

Part of the time-sense difference that Hunters have from other people leads to the "too many projects started, not enough finished" syndrome. Add to that the feeling almost all Hunters have that they're not living up to their potential, and you have a virtual guarantee that when people ask a Hunter to do something, she will say, "Yes."

This is another trap.

Most Hunters actually do, and complete, about half the work they think they can, provided the job is to be done to completion and is to be done right. I remember how shocked I was years ago when I asked my Farmer business partner in an herbal tea company if he'd take on a new project and he replied, "No, I just don't have the time."

"Make the time!" was my irate reply. How, after all, could somebody ever not have the time for something new? This request was only going to take him a few hours!

"I just don't have the time," he said with finality. "Sorry."

Prior to that I'd never said, "No, I just don't have the time" to anybody in my life, so far as I can remember. The concept hadn't even occurred to me. It was a great lesson learned from a brilliant business-man, although I still struggle with overcommitment.

So, learn to say "No." It doesn't mean you're less capable: it'll actu-ally make you more capable.

Live in the Now

When we remember back over our lives, time into childhood seems like a vast, colorless ocean, studded with sparkling jewels of crystal clear memory. That one incredible birthday party, the new bike, the wed-ding, that car accident, the day the dog died. Many of those crystals of memory aren't associated with any particular "high point"; they're just there. It's the everyday moments: sitting in the woods, or fishing, or rid-ing a bike in the country, or dinner three weeks ago Thursday.

This oddity of memory, that most things are a squishy gray but that there are little moments of "light" in there, used to fascinate me. What caused those memorable moments?

I believe I got the answer to that question from a meditation teacher I once had, a man named Kurt Stanley. Stanley said: "Most people spend every moment of every day thinking about the past or the future. They're reviewing their fears, recounting their joys, planning, thinking—in short, doing everything except noticing the fact that at that very moment they are alive."

After you read this paragraph, put down this book for a moment, look up and around you, and notice where you are: the smell of the air, the sounds, the color of the light. Feel your body. Pause for a moment from thinking about these words and notice your own aliveness.

If you did this successfully, the experience will become one of those little jewels of memory. I'm convinced that most people spend as little as five minutes a week actually "being alive in the here and now." All the rest of the time they're discussing with themselves the past or the future, instead of living in the present. (This is particularly true of the more hyperactive Hunters among us.)

Learn to set aside the thoughts and fears, let tomorrow worry about itself, and forgive the errors of the past. It's the essence of the Sermon on the Mount, and the best advice for living a Hunter's life that I've ever found.

Because the world of business is so complex, and every day is fraught with a thousand competitive pressures, problems, and opportunities, the temptation to live in the past or worry about the future is very strong. But those businesspeople who have prospered have usually learned how to plan for the future, but to do that planning in the "now"—and then to live each business day, one day at a time.

Learn to Forgive

The business world is a rough place. Competitors steal our clients, snatch our secrets, hire away our best people, and then attack us in their advertising. It's easy to build up animosities and even hatreds. There are many, many people in the business world who seem totally without ethics, and it's often difficult to not take personally the attacks on our companies.

On top of that, Hunters bring to the workplace their own unique pains of half-fulfilled dreams, parental upset over poor schoolwork, less than successful relationships, and persistent problems with organization and follow-through. These are all destructive to self-esteem, and make some people defensive, thin-skinned, afraid of criticism, or easy to upset.

But these angers and resentments are corrosive and time wasters of the worst type.

An old friend and psychologist confided in me, years ago, that he'd discovered "an amazingly powerful new therapeutic tool." He'd tried to tell a few of his peers about it and they'd scoffed, but with the patients he convinced to try it, it was life transforming.

Forgiveness was the tool, and of course my friend hadn't really discovered anything new. As long as you hold a grudge, carry an anger or a hurt, against anybody—including yourself—you're stuck to that pain, like a persistent piece of gum on your shoe. Forgiveness is not a weakness— it's a strength. It's a shedding of those pains and encumbrances.

My friend's technique was to have his patients close their eyes and visualize, one after another, all the people in their lives with whom they were angry. Then they were to silently say to each of those people, "I forgive you. You were wrong, and you hurt me, and now I forgive you." He then had them do it with all the things that they were hating themselves for, too.

Try it: it works.

Never Criticize, Complain, or Condemn

This is the first golden rule of the Dale Carnegie Course,* and it's brilliant. Most Hunters, because of their lifetime frustrations with accomplishment and follow-through, have learned an internal motivation system that involves self-criticism. Learning from mistakes is one of the rationalizations that adults with ADHD use to their benefit, but there's probably also a good chunk of early voices from a Hunter's childhood, reminding him that he didn't do his homework on time.

While this self-criticism may work for some people internally, it's a lousy way to supervise other people.

Criticism nearly always arouses hurt feelings, and makes people immediately want to justify their actions—diminishing, rather than increasing, the probability that they'll change the criticized behavior. Complaints sound whiny and useless; unless you have a specific recommendation for change, they're just viewed as a sign of weakness. And condemnation of others does nothing except destroy their morale.

Instead of catching people doing things wrong, a more effective management strategy is to catch them doing things right. This builds their morale, makes them want to do more, and gives them a sense of empowerment. In the past five years, we've given "I Caught You Doing

---

*Dale Carnegie Training, www.dalecarnegie.com, (800) 231-5800

Something Right" forms to over 15,000 businesspeople who've attended our seminars across the country, and many have reported back that when they use them, the results are dramatic.

Hunting for Success in Your Personal Life

Another useful hunt, and one that many Hunters are constantly engaged in (if the sales figures for self-help books are any measure), is for personal improvement. Learn speed-reading. Take night courses in a foreign language. Travel and learn about other countries and cultures. Volunteer to work with local philanthropic or religious organizations. Get into politics.

In addition to providing important business contacts, these activities all bring you back to the "centering" that's so necessary to keep your business goals on track with your purpose and personal goals.

Partner with Your Spouse and Family

Another area to hunt for success is in your relationships. If there's such a thing as a perfect marriage, I've never seen it: there's always something more we can do for and with our spouses. They are, after all, our most important support.

If you have children, try setting goals for yourself with regard to them. Don't try to set their goals (a common parental mistake): instead set your own goals for what you're going to teach them, or how many books you're going to read to them, or how well you can get to know them.

Sharing your business goals is a good way to show children how to set their own goals, and the process of developing family-based goals will help make you more centered and effective in your work.

Because of the apparently genetic nature of ADHD, odds are if you're a Hunter and have children, at least some of them have ADHD, too. This creates a special challenge for parents, as just parenting—in and of itself—is a hard job. Throw ADHD into the mix on both the parent's and child's side, and the household can dissolve into chaos.

This is where becoming more aware of impulsivity, and teaching that awareness to your children, is particularly important. The angry, unthinking answer; the snap decisions about punishment or consequences; the brush-off when kids need help with homework (it's as boring for parents as it is for kids!): all these can add up to a worsening of the child's problems around his own ADHD, and will damage parent-child relationships.

The principles in this book to help with ADHD aren't unique to business, and can be easily adapted to the home and to children, particularly in school. For example, the distraction-free zone in the office becomes the front row in the classroom, where the rest of the class can't be seen by the child. The importance of training employees properly applies equally to teaching children to do a job right the first time, be it mowing the lawn, doing their own laundry, or cleaning the garage. Learning self-awareness about ADHD issues translates to sharing insights about your own ADHD with your ADHD children, and listening carefully as they share their own experiences back. All take time, but it's important to push through your own natural impatience and commit to that time, so the child really learns what's expected of him. This also provides an opportunity for those positive and constructive interactions between parent and child that are so often lacking in modern life.

Set Spiritual Goals and Work toward Them Daily

This may sound corny to some, but I am firmly convinced that all human power comes from some spiritual source. And virtually every successful person I've ever talked with about this has a similar story to tell. They have found, in some form, a spiritual wellspring that they go to for strength and renewal.

Be it waking up in the morning and looking out the window and saying, "Thank you, God, for this day," or communing out in the woods with nature, or going to church, mosque, or synagogue regularly, these successful Hunters have all found their own personal way to touch the source of their life.

Explore spiritual options, and look for ways to build this into your life. Many businesspeople even bring this into their own business. While having a boss who's an evangelist for a particular sect may be disconcerting, having a company that supports good works can be inspiring. All of this must flow, though, from a sense of personal commitment, and that starts with you.

Making Decisions about Medication

Being a Hunter means that you may also have what psychiatrists and psychologists have defined as a "disorder." And for many people with ADHD, it truly is a problem: their inattentiveness has reduced their life to a shambles or destroyed relationships, or their search for high stimulation has led them into dangerous and possibly self-destructive territory.

Psychiatrists offer several medications (as mentioned in chapter 4) to diminish the symptoms of ADHD. These drugs increase focusing ability and help people control impulsive behavior, reducing their feelings of "drivenness."

Independent of business considerations, medication is an option you may want to examine if you're unhappy with, or having difficulty with, the way you are or your personal life is running. Taking medication for ADHD is no more an admission of failure than wearing glasses is to correct nearsightedness. And many people with ADHD find that their lives are in such a shambles that "putting on the glasses" of a medication is incredibly useful.

On the other hand, if you were only slightly nearsighted (and can thus see close-up detail more easily than normal-sighted people) and made your living as a jeweler (to extend the metaphor), you may find glasses less necessary or more trouble than they're worth. Matching your personality type to appropriate job functions may reduce the need for medication if your ADHD is not severe.

Give Some of Yourself to Others

It's been said that we get what we give. Finding your purpose, defining your goals, hunting to reach those goals, and enjoying the fruits of the hunt are the first four steps. But the final step is to share some of yourself—what and who you are, and what you know—with others.

Years ago at The Newsletter Factory, we started irregular luncheon meetings in which I'd share my knowledge of marketing and advertising with my employees. My goal was for everybody there to know what I knew—plus what they knew. The "classes" were optional, but most people attended, and we expanded them on occasion to have other members of the company share their knowledge as well.

So share what you know and what's worked for you. If this message, for example, has been useful to you, pass it along.

12

Enjoying the Fruits of the Hunt

Lives of great men all remind us
We can make our lives sublime
And, departing, leave behind us,
Footprints in the sands of time.

HENRY WADSWORTH LONGFELLOW,
A PSALM OF LIFE

What's Next?

Hunters thrive on stimulation. The first rough draft of this book was written during a week's vacation with my family in a seaside house on Harbor Island, South Carolina. The theory was that we'd spend a week there—on the seashore—with nothing to do and nowhere to go, and I'd relax. It sounded good in theory, but as I type these words, watching the surf pound the sand just a hundred yards in front of me, I must confess that the nine hours of writing I've done today is more gratifying to me than any amount of lying on the beach in the sun would have been.

I used to feel guilty that I was a workaholic. Now I understand that it's part of my basic mental and physical biochemistry, and I have learned to relax into it, rather than fight it. I've learned to build in family time, considering it a project right along with everything else, and—using the techniques in this book—have accomplished much (and, hopefully, have learned good lessons from my failures).

Many businesspeople have told me that they come to these same realizations. After reading self-help books that said they had to learn to become "Type B's" or to stop working so hard, they discovered that it was the work that was keeping them alive, keeping them vital.

Focus Your Energy

Goethe, the German poet-philosopher and author of Faust, said, "Until one is committed, there is hesitancy, the chance to draw back, always ineffectiveness." This is a profound—and almost metaphysical—truth. I've started many businesses, ventures, and projects in a half-hearted fashion, and none of those have succeeded. Most were the product of an impulse, an enthusiasm of the moment, that later died.

On the other hand, when a person totally commits herself to a project or enterprise, charging ahead with a clear and well-thought-out plan, doors that were unimaginable in the original brainstorming and planning start to fall open. Goethe observed this, and wrote "the moment one definitely commits oneself, then providence moves too. All sorts of things occur to help one that would never otherwise have occurred. A whole stream of events issues from the decision, raising in one's favor all manner of unforeseen incidents and meetings and material assistance, which no man could have dreamed would have come his way."

Since childhood I've wondered if this oddity—that commitment consistently creates changes in the external world—was a deep truth that expressed some law of nature, or if it was just that once our receiver is fine-tuned, we start noticing things that we might have otherwise ignored. Forty years of experience in the business world, though, have convinced me that Goethe was right: commitment has its own unexplainable magic, which always works. By focusing our energies on our goal, a previously invisible road appears before us that—if we follow it with enthusiasm—will bring us to our objective.

You Can Do It!

As the concept of ADHD and Hunterness grows and evolves, more and more of the millions of people who've wondered all their lives why some things are just so hard to do will gain relief and insight. Hopefully they'll even discover a new empowerment, new solutions for the difficulties in their lives, and new ways to become truly successful as Hunters in a business world.

With these tools to track business quarries, ADHD Hunters can build and maintain successful enterprises, or increase their success within existing companies or organizations. Since many of the suggestions in this book are counterintuitive for Hunters (after all, the business world isn't the jungle, as much as that metaphor is overused), you may find it useful to reread this book every year or two—just as a reminder and refresher.

Remember Goethe's words to us Hunters who follow him down the trail of time and life:

Whatever you can do or dream you can, begin it.
Boldness has genius, power and magic in it.
Begin it now.

Bibliography

American Psychiatric Association. *Tic Disorders.* Vol. 1, *Treatments of Psychiatric Disorders.* Washington, D.C.: American Psychiatric Association, 1989.

———. *Diagnostic and Statistical Manual of Mental Disorders.* 5th ed. Washington, D.C.: American Psychiatric Association, 2013.

Anderson, J. C., et al. "DSMIII Disorders in Preadolescent Children. Prevalence in a Large Sample from the General Population." *Archives of General Psychiatry* 44 (1987): 69–76.

Barkely, R. A., et al. "Development of a Multimethod Clinical Protocol for Assessing Stimulant Drug Response in Children with Attention Deficit Disorder." *Journal of Clinical Child Psychology* 17 (1988): 14–24.

———. *Hyperactive Children: A Handbook for Diagnosis and Treatment.* New York: Guilford, 1981.

———. "The Social Behavior of Hyperactive Children: Developmental Changes, Drug Effects, and Situational Variation." In *Childhood Disorders: Behavioral-developmental Approaches*, edited by R. J. McMahon and R. D. Peters. New York: Brunner/Mazel, 1985.

Bowen, Catherine Drinker. *The Most Dangerous Man in America: Scenes from the Life of Benjamin Franklin.* Boston: Little, Brown & Company, 1974.

Brown, Ronald T., et al. "Effects of Methylphenidate on Cardiovascular Responses in Attention Deficit Hyperactivity Disordered Adolescents." *Journal of Adolescent Health Care* 10 (1989): 179–183.

Buckley, W. F., Jr. *Overdrive: A Personal Documentary.* New York: Doubleday & Company, 1983.

Burdett, Osbert. *The Two Carlyles.* N.p, 1930. Reprinted 1980.

Campbell, Ian. *Thomas Carlyle.* N.p, 1975.

Crichton, Michael. *Travels.* New York: Alfred A. Knopf, 1988.

Clubbe, John, ed. *Froud's Life of Carlyle.* Columbus: Ohio State University Press, 1979.

Comings, D. E., et al. "The Dopamine D2 Receptor Locus as a Modifying Gene in Neuropsychiatric Disorders." *Journal of the American Medical Association* 266 (1991): 1793–1800.

Comings, D. E., and B. G. Comings. "Tourette's Syndrome and Attention Deficit Disorder with Hyperactivity: Are They Genetically Related?" *Journal of the American Academy of Child Psychiatry* 23 (1984): 138–146.

Diamond, Jared. "How Africa Became Black." *Discover,* February 1, 1994.

Doyle, Sir Arthur Conan. "The Sign of the Four." *Lippincott's Monthly Magazine,* 1890.

Einstein, Albert. *Out of My Later Years.* New York: Bonanza, 1956, 1990.

Evans, R. W., T. H. Clay, and C. T. Gualtieri. "Carbamazepine in Pediatric Psychiatry." *Journal of the American Academy of Child Psychiatry* 26 (1987): 2–8.

Farwell, Byron. *Burton: A Biography of Sir Richard Francis Burton.* London: Penguin, 1990.

Feingold, Benjamin. *Why Your Child Is Hyperactive.* New York: Random House, 1975.

Garber, Stephen W., Marianne Daniels Garber, and Robyn Freedman Spitzman. *If Your Child Is Hyperactive, Inattentive, Impulsive, Distractible . . . : Helping the ADD (Attention Deficit Disorder)/Hyperactive Child.* New York: Villard Books, 1990.

Getzels, Jacob, and Mihaly Csikszentmihaly. *The Creative Vision: A Longitudinal Study of Problem Finding in Art.* Wiley, 1976.

Gittelman Klein, Rachel. "Pharmacotherapy of Childhood Hyperactivity: An Update." In *Psychopharmacology: The Third Generation of Progress,* edited by Herbert Y. Meltzer. New York: Raven, 1987.

Goyette, C. H., C. K. Conners, and R. F. Ulrich. "Normative Data on Revised Conners Parent and Teacher Rating Scales." *Journal of Abnormal Child Psychology* 6 (1978): 221–36.

Greenhill, Laurence, et al. "Prolactin: Growth Hormone and Growth Responses in Boys with Attention Deficit Disorder and Hyperactivity Treated with Methylphenidate." *Journal of the American Academy of Child Psychiatry* 23 (1984): 58–67.

Hayes, Peter L. *Ernest Hemingway.* New York: Continuum, 1990.

Henker, B., and C. K. Whalen. "The Changing Faces of Hyperactivity: Retrospect and Prospect." In *Hyperactive Children: The Social Ecology of Identification and Treatment,* edited by B. A. Henker and C. K. Whalen. New York: Academic, 1980.

Josephson, Matthew. *Edison: A Biography.* New York: John Wiley & Sons, 1959, 1992.

Kelly, Kevin L., et al. "Attention Deficit Disorder and Methylphenidate: A Multistep Analysis of DoseResponse Effects on Children's Cardiovascular Functioning." *International Clinical Psychopharmacology* 3 (1988): 167–181.

Kinsbourne, Marcel. "Overfocusing: An Apparent Subtype of Attention Deficit-Hyperactivity Disorder." In *Pediatric Neurology: Behavior and Cognition of the Child with Brain Dysfunction,* edited by N. Amir, I. Rapin, and D. Branski. Basel, Switzerland: Karger, 1991.

———. "Overfocusing: Attending to a Different Drummer." *CHADDER* (CHADD Newsletter) 6, no. 1 (1991): 23–33.

Kinsbourne, M., and P. J. Caplan. *Children's Learning and Attention Problems.* Boston: Little, Brown and Company, 1979.

Klein, Rachel G., B. Landa, J. A. Mattes, and D. F. Klein. "Methylphenidate and Growth in Hyperactive Children. A Controlled Withdrawal Study." *Archives of General Psychiatry* 45 (1988): 1127–30.

Klein, Rachel G., and Salvatore Mannuzzo. "Hyperactive Boys Almost Grown Up: Methylphenidate Effects on Ultimate Height." *Archives of General Psychiatry* 45 (1988): 1131–34.

Kuczenski, R., et al. "Effects of Amphetamine, Methylphenidate and Apomorphine on Regional Brain Serotonin and 5Hydroxyindole Acetic Acid." *Psychopharmacology* 93 (1987): 329–335.

Lakein, Alan. *How to Get Control of Your Time and Life.* New York: New American Library, 1973.

LoPorto, Garret. *The DaVinci Method.* Concord, Mass.: Media for Your Mind, 2005.

Lorayne, Harry, and Jerry Lucas. *The Memory Book*. New York: Ballantine, 1986.

Manchester, William. *Portrait of a President*. New York: Little, Brown and Company, 1962.

McGuinness, Diane. "Attention Deficit Disorder, the Emperor's Clothes, Animal Pharm, and Other Fiction." In *The Limits of Biological Treatment for Psychological Distress*, edited by Seymour Fisher and Roger P. Greenberg. New York: Erlbaum, 1989.

———. *When Children Don't Learn*. New York: Basic Books, 1985.

Mendelsohn, Robert S., M.D. *How to Raise a Healthy Child . . . in Spite of Your Doctor*. Chicago: Contemporary Books, 1984.

Moss, Robert A., and Helen H. Dunlap. *Why Johnny Can't Concentrate*. New York: Bantam Books, 1990.

Murray, John B. "Psychophysiological Effects of Methylphenidate (Ritalin)." *Psychological Reports* 61 (1987): 315–336.

Peters, Tom, and Robert Waterman. *In Search of Excellence*. New York: Harper & Row, 1982.

Rapaport, J. L., et al. "Dextroamphetamine: Its Cognitive and Behavioral Effects in Normal and Hyperactive Boys and Normal Men." *Archives of General Psychiatry* 37 (1980): 933–43.

Rapport, M. D., et al. "Attention Deficit Disorder and Methylphenidate: A Multilevel Analysis of Doseresponse Effects on Children's Impulsivity Across Settings." *Journal of the American Academy of Child Psychiatry* 27 (1988): 60–69.

Safer, Daniel J., et al. "A Survey of Medication Treatment for Hyperactive/Inattentive Students." *Journal of the American Medical Association* 260 (1988): 2256–2258.

Satterfield, James H., Dennis P. Cantwell, Ann Schell, and Thomas Blaschke. "Growth of Hyperactive Children Treated with Methylphenidate." *Archives of General Psychiatry* 36 (1979): 212–217.

Satterfield, James H., Breena T. Satterfield, and Ann M. Schell. "Therapeutic Interventions to Prevent Delinquency in Hyperactive Boys." *Journal of the American Academy of Child Psychiatry* 26 (1987): 56–64.

Scarnati, Richard. "An Outline of Hazardous Side Effects of Ritalin (Methylphenidate)." *The International Journal of Addictions* 21 (1986): 837–841.

Shaffer, D., et al. "Neurological Soft Signs: Their Relationship to Psychiatric Disorder and Intelligence in Childhood and Adolescence." *Archives of General Psychiatry* 42 (1985): 342–51.

Sharma, Rajiv P., et al. "Pharmacological Effects of Methylphenidate on Plasma Homovanillic Acid and Growth Hormone." *Psychiatry Research* 32 (1990): 9–17.

Sokol, Mae S., et al. "Attention Deficit Disorder with Hyperactivity and the Dopamine Hypothesis: Case Presentations with Theoretical Background." *American Academy of Child and Adolescent Psychiatry* 1987: 428–433.

Sternberg, Robert J., and Todd L. Lubart. "Creating Creative Minds." *Phi Delta Kappa,* April, 1991, 608–614.

Stewart, A. "Severe Perinatal Hazards." In *Developmental Neuropsychiatry,* edited by M. Rutter. New York: Guilford, 1983.

Strauss, C. C., et al. "Overanxious Disorder: An Examination of Developmental Differences." *Journal of Abnormal Child Psychology* 16 (1988): 433–43.

Swanson, J. M., and M. Kinsboume. "The Cognitive Effects of Stimulant Drugs on Hyperactive Children." In *Attention and Cognitive Development,* edited by G. A. Hale and M. Lewis. New York: Plenum, 1979.

Taylor, E., et al. "Which Boys Respond to Stimulant Medication? A Controlled Trial of Methylphenidate in Boys with Disruptive Behaviour." *Psychology Med* 17 (1987): 121–43.

Ullmann, R. K., and E. K. Sleator. "Responders, Nonresponders, and Placebo Responders Among Children with Attention Deficit Disorder." *Clinical Pediatrics* 25 (1986): 594–99.

U.S. Congress. Senate. *Examination into the Causes of Hyperactive Children and the Methods Used for Treating These Young Children.* Joint Hearing before a Subcommittee on Health of the Committee on Labor and Public Welfare and the Subcommittee on Administrative Practice and Procedure of the Committee on the Judiciary of the United States Senate. 94th Cong., 1st sess., September 11, 1975.

Weiss, G., and L. T. Hechtman. *Hyperactive Children Grown Up: Empirical Findings and Theoretical Considerations.* New York: Guilford, 1986.

Weiss, Lynn. *Attention Deficit Disorder in Adults.* Dallas: Taylor Publishing, 1992.

Weizman, Ronit, et al. "Effects of Acute and Chronic Methylphenidate Administration of B-endorphin, Growth Hormone, Prolactin and Cortisol in Children with Attention Deficit Disorder and Hyperactivity." *Life Sciences* 40 (1987): 2247–2252.

Wender, Paul H. *Minimal Brain Dysfunction in Children.* New York: Wiley, 1971.

Whalen, C. K., et al. "A Social Ecology of Hyperactive Boys: Medication Effects in Structured Classroom Environments." *Journal of Applied Behavioral Analysis* 12 (1979): 65–81.

Wilson, John. *Thomas Carlyle: The Iconoclast of Modern Shams.* Originally published by Alexander Gardner, 1881.

Winn, Marie. *The PlugIn Drug.* New York: Bantam, 1978.

Wolkenberg, F. "Out of a Darkness." *New York Times Magazine,* October 11, 1987.

Recommended Reading

If you are looking for more information about what ADHD is and how to manage it in your life, I recommend starting with these books. These classics and updated classics will support you on your journey to develop your Hunter skills.

Attention Deficit Disorder in Adults. Lynn Weiss. Dallas: Taylor Publishing, 1992.

Delivered from Distraction: Getting the Most out of Life with Attention Deficit Disorder. Edward Hallowell and John Ratey. Rev ed. New York: Ballantine, 2005.

Driven to Distraction. Edward Hallowell, M.D., and John Ratey, M.D. New York: Pantheon Press, 1994.

How to Raise a Healthy Child . . . in Spite of Your Doctor. Robert S. Mendelsohn, M.D. Chicago: Contemporary Books, 1984.

If Your Child Is Hyperactive, Inattentive, Impulsive, Distractible . . . : Helping the ADD (Attention Deficit Disorder)/Hyperactive Child. Stephen W. Garber, Marianne Daniels Garber, and Robyn Freedman Spitzman. New York: Villard Books, 1990.

Why Johnny Can't Concentrate. Robert A. Moss and Helen H. Dunlap. New York: Bantam Books, 1990.

You Mean I'm Not Lazy, Stupid or Crazy?!: The Classic Self-Help Book for Adults with Attention Deficit Disorder. Rev. ed. Kate Kelly, Peggy Ramundo. New York: Scribner, 2006.

Index

ABC organizational strategy, 95–97
accepting the worst, 86–87
Adderall, 22
ADHD characteristics
    creativity, 32, 61–62
    from *Driven to Distraction,* 10–11
    from DSM-5 Fact Sheet, 8–10
    in DSM-IV vs. DSM-5, 8–9
    genetic causes of, 13, 14
    as hunter characteristics, 13–14
    never growing up, 37–38
    presentations of ADHD, 9–10,
        49–50
    in range of human experiences,
        6–8
    self-knowledge and, 18–19, 25
    two-edged nature of, 18
    in women, 49–50
agenda for meetings, 47
agricultural revolution, 12, 15–16
alcohol, 21, 91
alertness to danger, 13, 14
Alexander, Doug, 34
ambiguity in creative efforts, 33
Amiel, Barbara, 41

antidepressants, 23
Arenson, Mickey, 55
atomoxetine (Strattera), 22
Attention Deficit Disorder, 2

behaving how you want to feel, 84
Bey, Hamid, 85
books, motivational, 93
brain chemistry and ADHD, 20–21
breaking up big jobs, 101–2

caffeine, 21
Carnegie, Andrew, 55, 98
Carnegie, Dale, 62
CHADD, 8
Churchill, Winston, 2, 45
combined inattentive and
        hyperactive-impulsive
        presentation, 10
coming out about ADHD, 39–42
commitment, world changed by,
        111–12
creative jobs, 32–34
Creative Vision, The, 32–33
creativity, 32, 33, 61–62

Crichton, Michael, 33
criticizing, avoiding, 105–6
Csikszentmihaly, Mihaly, 33

DaVinci Method, The, 54
Dexedrine (dextroamphetamine), 22
diagnosis of ADHD, 41–42. *See also*
    ADHD characteristics
Diagnostic and Statistical Manual of
    Mental Disorders (DSM-5), 8
Dickinson, Emily, 61
diet, 91–92
diseases, hunter-gatherer
    susceptibility to, 15–16
Driven to Distraction, 10–11
drugs
    brain chemistry changed by, 20–21
    deciding about, 23–24, 108–9
    prescription, 22–24, 108–9
    self-medication with, 22
"DSM-5 Fact Sheet on ADHD,"
    8–10
DSM-IV vs. DSM-5, 8–9
Durant, Will, 28

Edison, Thomas, 2, 70
Edison Gene, The, 13
entrepreneurial survival tips, 95–106
entrepreneurs
    becoming a consultant to your
        company, 60
    businesses vs. jobs, 55–56
    franchise preparations, 56, 73–74
    franchisers, 56
    Hunters as, 3, 54–56
    number with adult ADHD, 1, 2,
        54

organizing a business, 57–59
small businesspersons vs., 2
starting a business, 61–66
workplace opportunities for, 28–29
exercise, 20, 92

fallback plan, 86–87
Farmers
    hiring as managers, 99–100
    Hunters compared to, 13–14
    intermixing with Hunters, 14
    reasons for large numbers of, 15–16
    responsibility for regular meetings,
        49
    See also Hunter-Farmer teams
fear, confronting, 88
feelings, listening to yours, 87
focus
    commitment for, 111–12
    maintaining in meetings, 47
    positive, 84–86
    for your business, 57
Ford, Henry, 2, 70
forgetfulness, overcoming, 89–91
forgiveness, learning, 104–5
Fosdick, Harry Emerson, 12
franchising, 56, 73–74, 76
Franklin, Ben, 1–2

genetic causes of ADHD, 13, 14
Getzels, Jacob, 33
goals
    matching to your purpose, 67–68
    for meetings, 46–47
    setting for your business, 70
    spiritual, 107–8
    writing down, 95

Goethe, 111, 112

Hallowell, Edward, 10, 17, 33, 100
high-stimulation jobs, 35–38
hiring the best, 98
horizontal problem-solving, 62
Hunter-Farmer teams, 30–31, 76,
    77–78
Hunters
    characteristics of, 13–14
    creativity of, 32, 61–62
    defined, 3
    as entrepreneurs, 3, 54–56
    Farmers compared to, 13–14
    intermixing with Farmers, 14
    management not a strength of, 31
    reasons for low numbers of, 15–16
    sales positions suited to, 29–30
    women with ADHD, 49–50
hunting societies, 12–13, 15–16
hunt preparations, 82
husband-wife teams, 77–80
    defining responsibilities, 80
    Hunter-Farmer couples, 77–78
    not taking work home, 78–79
    not using ADHD as an excuse,
        77–78
    respecting each other's opinions, 79
hyperactive-impulsive presentation,
    9–10

impulsiveness
    curbing at business startup, 65
    curbing before quitting, 66
    in Hunters vs. Farmers, 13, 14
    in relationships, 107
    workplace challenges with, 25–26

inattentive presentation, 9
incorporating your business, 74–75
International Wholesale Travel,
    72–73

James, William, 84
job descriptions, writing, 57–58
job pool, evaluating, 58
jobs. See entrepreneurs; workplace
Johnson, Samuel, 1

Kennedy, John F., 2, 45
Kennedy, Robert, 45
Kroc, Ray, 55, 70

Lambert, Joan, 50–51
listening to your feelings, 87
Longfellow, Henry Wadsworth, 110
LoPorto, Garret, 54

management, 31–32, 43–46, 99–100
Manchester, William, 45
manuals for your business, 59, 60
Marcus Aurelius, 17
marijuana, 21, 23, 25
market research, 71–72, 100
Maslow, Abraham, 68
Mastermind groups, 97
meddling, avoiding, 98–99
medications and therapies, 20–26
    alternative treatments, 24
    deciding about, 23–24, 108–9
    exercise, 20
    prescription drugs, 22–24, 108–9
    psychotherapy, 25
    self-medication with drugs, 21
meditation, 63–64

meetings, making productive, 46–49
memory
    jewels of, 103–4
    original awareness for, 89–90
    visualizations aiding, 90–91
methylphenidate (Ritalin), 22, 23, 24, 25
military careers, 35
monitoring the marketplace, 100
motivational books and tapes, 93

names, remembering, 89
needs, hierarchy of, 68
negative self-talk, 83, 88
Newsletter Factory, The, 63
"No," learning to say, 102–3
now, living in the, 103–4
nutrition, 91–92

off-baseline individuals, 7
Olson, Tillie, 6
organizing
    ABC strategy for, 95–97
    business organization steps, 57–59
    for franchising, 56
original awareness, 89

pacing yourself, 100–101
parenting, 50–51, 106–7
partnerships
    caveats for, 75–76
    husband-wife teams, 77–80
    See also Hunter-Farmer teams
Pascal, 39
performance evaluation forms, 59
personal improvement, 106
pilots with ADHD, 35–36

pocket recorders, 64–65
Pope, Alexander, 20
positive focus, 84–86
prescription drugs, 22–24, 108–9
presentations of ADHD, 9–10, 49–50
problem-solving approaches, 62
procrastination, intentional, 66
professors with ADHD, 17–18, 34
profiling job skills, 58
psychotherapy, 25
purpose, finding yours, 67–69

quiet time, 63–64

Ratey, John, 10, 17, 100
recording your ideas, 64–65
relationships, success in, 106–7
responsibilities
    defining in partnerships, 76, 80
    job descriptions, 57–58
    performance evaluation forms, 59
    for regular meetings, 49
risk taking by Hunters, 14
Ritalin (methylphenidate), 22, 23, 24, 25
Roy, John, 84–85

sales, 29–32
saying "No," 102–3
Scott, Robert Falcon, 54
self-actualization, 68–69
self-knowledge, need for, 18–19, 25
self-medication with drugs, 21
self-talk, overcoming negative, 83, 88
sexual challenges, 25
sharing your knowledge, 109

Shelley, Mary, 67
skydiving, 37
smartphone apps, 65
specialization by farmers, 16
spiritual goals, 107–8
Sprayberry Travel, 72–73
starting a business, 61–66
    choosing the business, 61–63
    company structure, 74–76
    curbing impulsiveness, 65–66
    finding your purpose, 67–69
    franchise preparations, 56, 73–74
    husband-wife teams, 77–80
    incorporating, 74–75
    market research, 71–72
    purchasing franchises, 76
    recording your ideas, 64–65
    setting and reaching goals, 70
    startup money and success, 55
    usefulness criteria for, 63–64, 73
Stein, Mark, 18, 26
stimulants, 21, 22, 23
Strattera (atomoxetine), 22
structure
    for meetings, 48
    for your company, 74–76
subtypes (presentations), 9–10
success
    in management jobs, 43–46
    in meetings, 46–49
    not prevented by ADHD, 17–18
    in personal improvement, 106
    in relationships, 106–7
    self-knowledge needed for, 18–19
    startup money and, 55
success preparations
    accepting the worst, 86–87

behaving how you want to feel, 84
confronting fear, 88
diet and exercise, 91–92
listening to your feelings, 87
motivational books and tapes, 93
overcoming forgetfulness, 89–91
overcoming negative self-talk, 83, 88
positive focus, 84–86
rituals for, 82
sugar and sweets, 91
summary of business operation, 59

tapes, motivational, 93
Tennyson, Alfred, Lord, 82, 94
thinking, positive, 84–86
"30 Best Apps for ADHD Minds," 65
time management, 100–101
time sense, 13, 14
training employees, 101
travel agency business, 71–73
Travels, 33
trends in ailments, 41
Type A personality, 91–92, 110–11

unincorporated partnerships, 75

vertical problem-solving, 62
victimization, cult of, 41
visualizations as memory aids, 90–91

women with ADHD, 49–50
workplace
    avoiding criticizing, 105–6
    avoiding meddling, 98–99
    breaking up big jobs, 101–2

businesses vs. jobs, 55–56

coming out about ADHD in, 39–42

coworker relationships, 42–43

creative jobs, 32–34

entrepreneurs in companies, 28–29

high-stimulation jobs, 35–38

Hunter-Farmer teams, 30–31

impulsiveness in, 25–26

learning forgiveness, 104–5

learning to say "No," 102–3

making meetings productive, 46–49

management jobs, 31–32, 43–46

Mastermind groups, 97

men vs. women with ADHD in, 49–50

sales positions, 29–32

training employees, 101

working parents, 50–51

See also entrepreneurs

worst, accepting, 86–87

writers with ADHD, 32, 33–34

About the Author

Thom Hartmann has more than forty years of experience as an international entrepreneur—he has started projects on four continents and built up and sold seven companies. He was also the executive director of a residential treatment facility and school for children with ADHD and other disorders, the administrator of an international relief charity in Germany, and helped create and build a hospital and famine relief center in Uganda. In these capacities, and as a business consultant for nearly twenty years, he has worked with thousands of ADHD children and adults.

Formerly president of The Newsletter Factory in Atlanta, Georgia, he taught seminars across the United States on marketing with newsletters, and gave speeches on other aspects of marketing and business, as well as on attention deficit hyperactivity disorder.

On CompuServe in the 1980s and 1990s, Hartmann ran the Attention Deficit Disorder Forum (then the world's largest attention deficit hyperactivity support group, open twenty-four hours a day and with tens of thousands of members—including scores of psychiatrists and psychologists—in all fifty states and over a dozen foreign countries).

Currently he lives on a boat and does both radio and TV talk shows in Washington, D.C., where his need for stimulation is only rarely not met.

Books of Related Interest

ADHD and the Edison Gene
A Drug-Free Approach to Managing the Unique Qualities of Your Child
by Thom Hartmann

Walking Your Blues Away
How to Heal the Mind and Create Emotional Well-Being
by Thom Hartmann

The Prophet's Way
A Guide to Living in the Now
by Thom Hartmann

The Crack in the Cosmic Egg
New Constructs of Mind and Reality
by Joseph Chilton Pearce
Foreword by Thom Hartmann

The Biology of Transcendence
A Blueprint of the Human Spirit
by Joseph Chilton Pearce

The Heart-Mind Matrix
How the Heart Can Teach the Mind New Ways to Think
by Joseph Chilton Pearce
Foreword by Robert Sardello

The Neurofeedback Solution
How to Treat Autism, ADHD, Anxiety, Brain Injury, Stroke, PTSD, and More
by Stephen Larsen, Ph.D.

Children of the Fifth World
A Guide to the Coming Changes in Human Consciousness
by P. M. H. Atwater, L.H.D.

INNER TRADITIONS • BEAR & COMPANY
P.O. Box 388
Rochester, VT 05767
1-800-246-8648
www.InnerTraditions.com

Or contact your local bookseller